WINNING IN SMALL CLAIMS COURT MADE E-Z

MADE E-Z PRODUCTS, Inc.

Deerfield Beach, Florida / www.MadeE-Z.com

Winning In Small Claims Court Made E-Z™
Copyright 2000 Made E-Z Products, Inc.
Printed in the United States of America

MADE E-Z
PRODUCTS

384 South Military Trail
Deerfield Beach, FL 33442
Tel. 954-480-8933
Fax 954-480-8906

http://www.MadeE-Z.com

1 2 3 4 5 6 7 8 9 10   CPC   R 10 9 8 7 6 5 4 3 2

This publication is designed to provide accurate and authoritative information in regard to subject matter covered. It is sold with the understanding that neither the publisher nor author is engaged in rendering legal, accounting, or other professional services. If legal advice or other expert assistance is required, the services of a competent professional should be sought. From: *A Declaration of Principles jointly adopted by a Committee of the American Bar Association and a Committee of Publishers.*

Winning In Small Claims Court Made E-Z™

Important Notice

Limited warranty and disclaimer

This self-help product is intended to be used by the consumer for his/her own benefit. It may not be reproduced in whole or in part, resold or used for commercial purposes without written permission from the publisher. In addition to copyright violations, the unauthorized reproduction and use of this product to benefit a second party may be considered the unauthorized practice of law.

This product is designed to provide authoritative and accurate information in regard to the subject matter covered. However, the accuracy of the information is not guaranteed, as laws and regulations may change or be subject to differing interpretations. Consequently, you may be responsible for following alternative procedures, or using material or forms different from those supplied with this product. It is strongly advised that you examine the laws of your state before acting upon any of the material contained in this product.

As with any matter, common sense should determine whether you need the assistance of an attorney. We urge you to consult with an attorney, qualified estate planner, or tax professional, or to seek any other relevant expert advice whenever substantial sums of money are involved, you doubt the suitability of the product you have purchased, or if there is anything about the product that you do not understand including its adequacy to protect you. Even if you are completely satisfied with this product, we encourage you to have your attorney review it.

Neither the author, publisher, distributor nor retailer are engaged in rendering legal, accounting or other professional services. Accordingly, the publisher, author, distributor and retailer shall have neither liability nor responsibility to any party for any loss or damage caused or alleged to be caused by the use of this product.

Copyright Notice

The purchaser of this guide is hereby authorized to reproduce in any form or by any means, electronic or mechanical, including photocopying, all forms and documents contained in this guide, provided it is for non-profit, educational or private use. Such reproduction requires no further permission from the publisher and/or payment of any permission fee.

The reproduction of any form or document in any other publication intended for sale is prohibited without the written permission of the publisher. Publication for nonprofit use should provide proper attribution to Made E-Z Products.

Table of contents

How to use this guide

The Made E-Z™ guides can help you achieve an important legal objective conveniently, efficiently and economically. But it is important to properly use this guide if you are to avoid later difficulties.

◆ Carefully read all information, warnings and disclaimers concerning the legal forms in this guide. If after thorough examination you decide that you have circumstances that are not covered by the forms in this guide, or you do not feel confident about preparing your own documents, consult an attorney.

◆ Complete each blank on each legal form. Do not skip over inapplicable blanks or lines intended to be completed. If the blank is inapplicable, mark "N/A" or "None" or use a dash. This shows you have not overlooked the item.

◆ Always use pen or type on legal documents—never use pencil.

◆ Avoid erasures and "cross-outs" on final documents. Use photocopies of each document as worksheets, or as final copies. All documents submitted to the court must be printed on one side only.

◆ Correspondence forms may be reproduced on your own letterhead if you prefer.

◆ Whenever legal documents are to be executed by a partnership or corporation, the signatory should designate his or her title.

◆ It is important to remember that on legal contracts or agreements between parties all terms and conditions must be clearly stated. Provisions may not be enforceable unless in writing. All parties to the agreement should receive a copy.

◆ Instructions contained in this guide are for your benefit and protection, so follow them closely.

◆ You will find a glossary of useful terms at the end of this guide. Refer to this glossary if you encounter unfamiliar terms.

◆ Always keep legal documents in a safe place and in a location known to your spouse, family, personal representative or attorney.

Introduction to Winning In Small Claims Court Made E-Z™

The cost of hiring an attorney has skyrocketed in recent years. Long delays, document and witness costs, and the inaccessibility of the legal system to the average person, have also increased dramatically. The Small Claims Court system is designed to swiftly settle civil cases involving small amounts of money, making a civil suit more practical and affordable.

This user-friendly guide provides a step-by-step introduction to the Small Claims Court system. You'll learn how to decide if you have a case and if so, how to represent yourself in court—who to sue, how to prepare and file your case, and what to expect when you go to court. Now every citizen, whether plaintiff or defendant, can assert his right to have his grievances heard and wrongs set right—the E-Z way!

What is Small Claims Court?

1

Chapter 1

What is Small Claims Court?

What you'll find in this chapter:

➠ When to use Small Claims Court

➠ When you should sue

➠ Why you should take it to court

➠ Preparing your case

➠ What to expect in court

DEFINITION

Small Claims Court is a state court that hears civil cases, or non-criminal cases that protect private rights or recover monetary damages for wrongs suffered. You can't use Small Claims Court to get a divorce, change your name, or stop the city from building a mall on your neighborhood park. Small Claims Court hears cases that involve a payment of money or services: landlord/tenant disputes, personal injury and property damage claims, or claims for unpaid bills, for example.

note Small Claims Court is user-friendly and relatively inexpensive.

The amount of damages sought rarely exceeds a few thousand dollars, procedures are simple and lawyers are unnecessary. There is no legal terminology nor difficult rules to follow. Claims are usually heard within a month of filing, and the hearing itself usually takes only 15 minutes.

Small Claims Court varies in minor ways from state to state and may be called a variety of names, from Justice of the Peace Courts to Magistrate Courts. Most concepts discussed in this guide apply to every state, but your local laws are important. Go to your local courthouse and ask the clerk of the Small Claims Court for the court procedures for your district. Also refer to the state-by-state guidelines in the Appendix.

Should you sue?

How do you know whether Small Claims Court is the legal route you should take? Determine if the results you are likely to achieve exceed the time, cost and effort you are likely to expend. To help you do that, ask yourself these 10 questions:

1) Do I have the time to properly prepare and file a lawsuit? Can I take time off work to attend a hearing?

2) Do I have the money to file? What are the Small Claims filing and service fees in my state?

3) Can I prove that the person I am suing is responsible for my loss and should be held legally accountable?

4) Am I filing within the time allowed?

5) Am I filing within the proper geographical jurisdiction?

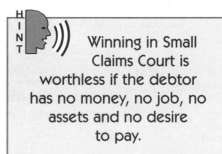

HINT Winning in Small Claims Court is worthless if the debtor has no money, no job, no assets and no desire to pay.

6) Am I suing the correct party?

7) Is my case likely to be more difficult because the person I am suing is out of state?

8)   Can I provide the necessary information to find the person I am suing?

9)   Have I made an effort to compromise and settle the case?

10) Can I collect on a judgment? Will my lawsuit pay off?

Reasons to sue

Many kinds of cases are found in Small Claims Courts.

• *Property damage*

When the negligent or intentional acts of another result in damaged property, your right to use that property has been damaged by those actions and you can sue to recover your loss.

A dry cleaner who stains your favorite suit provides the classic example of a property damage claim. Property damage claims can also arise from automobile accidents, construction site mishaps or a friend's negligence while using your borrowed lawn mower.

• *Personal injury*

If you suffer personal injury due to the intentional or negligent behavior of another, that person is legally liable for the costs of those injuries.

note Perhaps the greatest number of personal injury claims arise from automobile accidents or slip-and-fall claims brought against the local supermarket or neighborhood restaurant.

If you are injured because of the negligence of another and you can prove that negligence—

whether it's because you received stitches after stepping on a rake your neighbor left lying in your driveway or because you were taken to the emergency room after a brick fell on your head as you walked past a construction site—you can recover money for the damages you incurred.

• *Contract dispute*

When someone breaks a valid contract with you, whether written or implied, and you lose money, you can sue that person to recover your loss.

If you can document that you entered into a valid contract with another, that the contract was broken, and that you lost money as a result, you can recover your loss in Small Claims Court.

> *note* Contracts take many shapes and forms, and they are not always in writing.

• *Defective product*

If you are injured while using a defective product, you may recover damages from the manufacturer.

You may be familiar with some of the more well-known suits that fall under this category, such as the Dalkon Shield and Ford Pinto lawsuits. In both cases the manufacturers lost big bucks as a result of defective products.

• *Breach of warranty*

If you lose money because an express or implied warranty is breached, you can sue to recover your loss.

> If a product you have purchased doesn't work properly, you can recover monetary losses—even without an express warranty.

A breach of warranty suit usually applies to new products, although some used products, such as automobiles and major appliances, may come with short-term, limited warranties.

• *Violation of consumer protection laws*

If your consumer rights are violated and you suffer monetary loss, you may be entitled to recover.

For example, a store advertising a great sale doesn't have the advertised item, or it's not of the quality advertised. The store then gets you to buy a more expensive model. But since you are protected by law against this "bait-and-switch" tactic, you have remedy in Small Claims Court.

You do not have to specify what law is being broken when you take a case to Small Claims Court, but it is good to know under which area of law your case falls. It will help you in convincing the court to find in your favor. The judge will decide whether your case meets any of the criteria for suit outlined above. You must simply present the facts and show proof that you have lost money and that you are suing the right party.

Win by avoiding Small Claims Court

2

Chapter 2

Win by avoiding Small Claims Court

What you'll find in this chapter:

➠ Why you should try to settle out of court

➠ The Covenant Not to Sue

➠ The first Demand Letter

➠ Strategies for settling out of court

➠ How to combat excuses

Don't file your small claims case too hastily. You can be a winner in Small Claims Court by resolving your dispute before it gets to court. *Litigation should be a last resort.* Try one or several of these settlement methods first:

Compromise

Most adversaries don't settle only because they've never been asked to. Ask! If you each compromise a little, you may quickly settle the matter. If you do reach a compromise, put it in writing for both parties. Use the Covenant Not to Sue form contained in this guide (a sample is on the next page). If you are unable to reach a compromise, put that in writing as proof in court of your good-faith attempt to settle.

An offer of compromise, either oral or written, never binds you to the amount you offer if the compromise is rejected. Telling your opponent that you will accept $500 of the $750 you feel is due doesn't stop you from suing for the $750 if the offer is refused.

COVENANT NOT TO SUE

FOR GOOD AND VALUABLE CONSIDERATION RECEIVED, the undersigned being the holder of an actual, asserted or prospective claim against Shirley Smith , arising from (describe obligation or claim):

Return of a $500 deposit toward the rental of an apartment at 20 Elm Street, SomeCity, SomeState, so the apartment could be rented to someone else,

do hereby covenant that I/~~we~~ shall not commence or maintain any suit thereon against said party, whether at law or in equity, provided nothing in this agreement shall constitute a release of this or any other party thereto.

This covenant shall be binding upon and inure to the benefit of the parties, their successors, assigns and executors, administrators, personal representatives and heirs.

The undersigned affixes and seals this 30th day of June , 2010 .

Signed in the presence of:

Wilma Witness
_____
Witness

Alison Doe
_____

State of SomeState
County of SomeState

On June 30, 2010 , before me, Nick Notary , personally appeared Alison Doe , personally known to me (or proved to me on the basis of satisfactory evidence) to be the person(s) whose name(s) is/are subscribed to the within instrument and acknowledged to me that he/she/they executed the same in his/her/their authorized capacity(ies), and that by his/her/their signature(s) on the instrument the person(s), or the entity upon behalf of which the person(s) acted, executed the instrument.
Witness my hand and official seal.

Signature *Nick Notary*_____

My commission expires: _____   Affiant __✔ Known _____ Produced ID
                                       Type of ID _____
                                                                 (Seal)

First Demand Letter

If compromise fails, then send your adversary a Demand Letter briefly reviewing the entire dispute. An organized and logical letter is most valuable in Small Claims Court. Get right to the point. Your Demand Letter should be less than two pages long. Since its purpose is to resolve the problem, write your Demand Letter tactfully. Politely and firmly demand that payment be made or the contract honored. Without threatening, set a time limit for action to avoid suit. Is your opponent a business? Mention the Better Business Bureau or other influential business organizations.

> **HINT**
> Send your Demand Letter by certified mail, return receipt requested, so you have proof that it was received.

A sample Demand Letter follows. *No form letter of demand is included in this guide* because every case is different, and your Demand Letter must reflect your case. Use the sample Demand Letter on the following page as a guide in writing your own.

> **E-Z TIP**
> Keep copies of your Demand Letter, including one for the court if the case is filed.

DEMAND LETTER

Date: June 15, 2010
To: Shirley Smith
          18 Elm Street
          SomeCity, SomeState 99999

Dear Ms. Smith:

On June 10, 2010, I paid to you a $500 cash deposit to rent the apartment at 20 Elm Street. You accepted the money, and I began to make arrangements to move into the apartment by July 1. These arrangements included breaking my current lease, which cost me a $500 deposit, and rerouting utility services, which cost me $40 in lost wages and an additional $150 in reconnection charges.

While you returned my $500 cash deposit on June 14, 2010, I am still out $690 in costs I would not have incurred had you not breached our verbal contract. In addition, I now have 15 days to find a new apartment, as my current landlord has already rented my apartment to someone else.

I am asking that you either honor our verbal agreement immediately or pay me $690 to cover the additional costs I incurred as a result of your action. Please respond to me at the address or phone number below.

Very truly,

Alison Doe
14 Oak Street, #1
SomeCity, SomeState 99999
(123) 456-7890 (evenings)

Certified mail/return receipt requested

Telephone

A telephone call to your adversary may result in an immediate resolution. Keep the call businesslike and pleasant so the other party can voice his or her reasons for failing to pay. Have your key arguments before you when you call, identify yourself and your business, and be sure to speak directly to the debtor (some states impose liability for disclosing this kind of information to the wrong person).

Mediation

Many states encourage meeting with a professional mediator before setting a court date. Find out if your state has such a program. A third party may be just what you need to come to an agreement that seems fair to all. Participation in some programs binds you to follow the mediator's decision. Other programs are optional, allowing you to continue your case in Small Claims Court if you are dissatisfied with the mediator's decision.

Settlement

If you settle after you have filed in Small Claims Court, detail the settlement terms in writing. Then notify the court that you will not be appearing at your hearing. If your settlement involves installment payments,

The Covenant Not to Sue provides an ideal way to document your settlement agreement.

go to court on the appointed date, present your agreement and have the judge issue a judgment that coincides with your settlement agreement. Alternatively, a *Stipulation of Settlement* allows you to specify that a judgment won't be entered against the debtor as long as the payments are current. If the debt then goes unpaid (that is, if the defendant defaults), you can collect your money by enforcing the judgment without need to litigate the matter in court. A sample Stipulation of Settlement follows.

In the County Court

In and for SomeCounty **County,** SomeState

Harry Smith	Case No.: Division: **Civil**
Plaintiff,	
v.	
John Doe	
Defendant.	

STIPULATION OF SETTLEMENT

The plaintiff, Harry Smith , and the **defendant,** John Doe , hereby agree that this claim is settled for the sum **of $ 750.00** , to be paid on or before December 31 , 2010 to **plaintiff at 81 Some**Street, SomeCity, SomeState 99999 **or as follows:**

Upon payment, Plaintiff and Defendant shall **be released from** any liability relating to this dispute.

Plaintiff is entitled to judgment without further **notice in the event** of default in payment by defendant.

Dated: November 1, 2010

Harry Smith
Plaintiff

John Doe
Defendant

Strategies for settling out of court

Follow these guidelines when settling out of court:

- Begin by demanding immediate payment in full.

- If that fails, insist on large installment payments. The first payment should be half the debt, with smaller payments thereafter.

- Ask that the problem be resolved. If you want the company to repair your roof, say so. Speak directly to the person who makes such decisions.

- Make the idea of a settlement sound appealing. An out-of-court settlement is a win-win situation.

- If successful, send a confirmation letter restating the terms of the settlement.

- DO NOT threaten. Hostility is self-defeating and also unnecessary. You always have the option of filing in Small Claims Court.

- DO NOT lie.

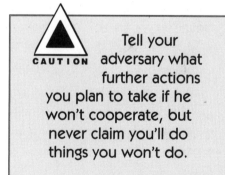

CAUTION Tell your adversary what further actions you plan to take if he won't cooperate, but never claim you'll do things you won't do.

How to combat excuses

If money is due you, don't let lame excuses keep the other party from paying up. Here are excuses you might hear and responses that will get you your money:

◆ *"The check is in the mail."* Explain that you will give the check one week to arrive, and that you will take immediate action if it does not.

◆ *"I lost my job."* Suggest an installment plan, preferably one that coincides with his or her unemployment check or other periodic income.

◆ *"My ex-husband/wife was supposed to pay this."* Divorce has no effect on your claim. If both parties were obligated to pay you money, both parties are still obligated.

Establishing your claim

Chapter 3

Establishing your claim

What you'll find in this chapter:

⟹ Why the size of your claim matters

⟹ Claim splitting

⟹ Deciding what type of claim you have

⟹ Equitable relief and specific performance

⟹ The statute of limitations

Claims too large or too small

There is such a thing as too small a claim, even for Small Claims Court. If your loss is less than $250, it is not advisable to pursue it. Most judges view suits with very small losses as a waste of time and taxpayer dollars.

Each state sets its own "jurisdictional limit," above which you must take your claim to a larger, more traditional court. The Appendix in this guide can be used as a benchmark, but check your local laws.

You may want to reduce the amount of your claim to keep the case in Small Claims Court. However, if you reduce your claim you forever waive the right to pursue the remaining amount in a second lawsuit, and you cannot sue the same person twice for the same claim.

Claim splitting

In some cases you can split your claim into two or more smaller lawsuits and keep both claims in Small Claims Court. However, you can sue the same person with multiple claims only if each claim is based on a separate legal theory. For example, you may decide your $3,000 lawsuit is actually a $2,000 claim for breach of contract and a $1,000 claim for property damage. Of course, a judge may disagree and allow only one case, which means you can recover only part of your loss.

Deciding your type of claim

The following guidelines can be used for computing certain types of claims:

Contract disputes

Compute the difference between the amount you were supposed to receive under the contract and the amount you actually received. Example: If X was to paint Y's house for $1,000 and Y paid only $750, X has a claim against Y for $250.

In a breach of contract case, the "plaintiff," or person bringing the suit, must "mitigate the damages," or take all reasonable steps to limit the amount of damage suffered. Example: If a landlord is suing a tenant for breach of a lease (contract), the landlord must try to re-rent the apartment for the remainder of the lease. If successful, he must then deduct the recovered rent from his damages. If he tries but fails, the damages remain the same.

> **HINT**
> If the contract specifically included interest, include interest due in the amount you sue for.

Property damage

Your claim here is usually for the amount of money it would take to fix the damaged item. To prove the actual value of your property, obtain written estimates and/or have an authority testify in court. Example: If your car is hit and repair is estimated at $500, your claim is for $500. However, if the repair cost exceeds the fair market value of the car, your claim can only be for the fair market value minus its value after the damage. Example: Your car was worth $1,000 and is now worth $100. If repairs cost $1,200 (or more than the car's pre-accident value), your claim would be for $900 (the $1,000 pre-accident market value minus $100 post-accident market value).

Clothing and other durable products

Cases involving clothing and other depreciable products, which are common in Small Claims Court, have their own rules. The judge will consider how much the item cost originally, what proportion of its life was consumed and whether the item has any remaining value or is completely ruined.

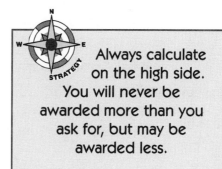

Always calculate on the high side. You will never be awarded more than you ask for, but may be awarded less.

If the item was new at the time of the accident, sue for its full value. Otherwise, sue for an amount that reflects how useful it was when damaged. Example: The cleaner ruins your new $500 coat. Sue for $500. But if the coat is two years old and would last only another two years, sue for 50 percent of its value, or $250.

Personal injury

Personal injury damages usually exceed the jurisdictional limit of Small Claims Court, but small personal injury cases are found in Small Claims Court.

Here, compute the total of out-of-pocket expenses, loss of pay for missing work, damage to property and any pain and suffering.

 You cannot collect money in court if you have recovered from a third party. Example: If your insurance company paid your medical bill or your employer paid for your missed work days, you can't sue for those costs.

Pain and suffering

Pain and suffering is generally calculated as three to four times your of out-of-pocket expenses. If your out-of-pocket expenses are $250, $1,000 for pain and suffering is reasonable.

Emotional distress

Emotional distress is any non-physical injury, and is difficult to prove. Example: If your neighbor plays loud music at 4 a.m. every day, you may eventually suffer emotional distress that you can sue for.

What factors determine how much you may be rewarded for emotional distress?

- How obnoxious was your opponent's behavior?

- How long has the distressing behavior continued?

Keep a copy of each written demand, and send your letters certified mail, return receipt requested.

- How often have you asked your opponent to stop?

- How does the judge view the behavior and your suffering?

Costs

Costs may include filing fees, subpoena fees for witnesses, and service fees, but do not include costs for any missed work or transportation to and from court.

> **HINT** Although you may be awarded the costs of taking your case to Small Claims Court, do not include those costs in your suit. The judge does this when he or she issues a judgment.

Bad checks

Some statutes allow you extra damages beyond the amount of your financial injury if you receive a bad check or one on which payment was erroneously stopped. You must first allow the bad check issuer the allotted time (review state laws) to make good on it. If that does not occur, you can sue for the amount of the check plus a penalty, or extra damages.

> **note** Your state statute will determine the penalty allowed, but triple the amount of the check is typical, with minimum and maximum limits.

Equitable relief

You may want non-monetary relief. Example: You want your roof fixed. Make that demand in your lawsuit (mention the item's value as well). Not all states allow equitable relief in Small Claims Court (check local laws), but there may be limited opportunities for equitable relief in your state. These include:

DEFINITION

- *Rescission* is a request to cancel (or rescind) a contract and return any money paid. This is commonly used when a contract is grossly unfair, fraudulent, based on an important factual error, induced by duress or undue influence or when one party does not receive what was promised through the fault of the other party.

DEFINITION

- *Restitution* restores two contracting parties to their original positions. Example: You sell your car and never get paid. The judge may order your car returned to you in lieu of payment.

DEFINITION

- *Reformation* rewrites a contract to meet the intent of the parties. It is most common when an agreement is drafted incorrectly, perhaps by omitting or misstating a term or condition.

Specific performance

When money damages alone cannot adequately compensate the plaintiff, the judge may award a specific equitable remedy. Example: You contract to purchase an antique car and the seller breaches the contract. The judge may order that the car be sold to you, as you have no opportunity to buy a comparable car on the open market.

The statute of limitations

Always sue as soon as possible after a dispute arises, because each state has a "statute of limitations" or time limit within which a lawsuit must be filed. Although this limit varies, it usually begins the day the disputed event occurs and lasts at least a year. Once the time limit passes, you lose the right to make a claim.

A defendant effectively waives the statute of limitations by asking for more time or other forbearances in paying the claim, as such an agreement in writing re-establishes the debt. The statute of limitations is also *tolled*, or suspended, if the

> HINT The local statute of limitations can be found in most public and law libraries under "Limitations" or "Statute of Limitations."

DEFINITION

defendant is in prison, lives out of state, is legally insane, or a minor. The time limit begins again when the defendant's impediment is removed.

If you are the defendant and the statute of limitations has expired (or some other legal requirement has not been met), *speak up*. Don't expect the court to establish your defenses. If, as a defendant, you must file a written request prior to the hearing date, that is an appropriate time to point out that the claim is barred by the statute of limitations.

HOT spot If the government is the party being sued, it must be notified of your claim immediately. If your dispute involves a city, county or state, check local laws.

Who and where to sue

4

Chapter 4

Who and where to sue

What you'll find in this chapter:

➭ Who may sue in court

➭ How the plaintiff files the suit

➭ Choosing the right party to sue

➭ Where to file your suit

➭ Out-of-jurisdiction defendants

Who can file a suit?

You can file a suit if you are of legal age and have not been declared mentally incompetent in court.

Lawyers may represent the plaintiff or defendant in most Small Claims Courts, but check local laws for exceptions. Most states also allow collection agencies (termed "assignees") to represent a plaintiff. Emancipated minors, or those under 18 who are no longer in the custody of their parents, may file a suit. Otherwise, minors must be represented by a parent or legal guardian, or a court may appoint a guardian ad litem to represent a minor. A prisoner may, in some states, file a claim by mail and waive a personal appearance.

note
A number of people with similar circumstances may band together to file a class action suit, but this seldom occurs in Small Claims Court. Yet a community dispute concerning pollution or noise, in which a large number of people sharing a particular grievance want to sue the same party, may find Small Claims Court their answer.

Who files the suit?

- If the plaintiff is an individually owned business, the owner's name and the business name must be listed on the claim: John Doe doing business as ABC Painting.

- If the plaintiff is a partnership, only one partner need sign the claim form.

- If the plaintiff does business under a fictitious name rather than the individual or partners' names, papers must be filed as: ABC Painting, a partnership, and John Doe and Jane Smith, individually.

- If the plaintiff is a corporation, the papers must be signed by an officer or a person authorized to file claims for the corporation.

HOT spot State regulations for filing on behalf of a corporation vary; check local laws.

- If the plaintiff is an unincorporated association, the papers must be filed in the name of the association and the officer representing it.

- If the plaintiff is a government agency, the papers must be filed by someone so authorized.

- If the claim concerns damage to an automobile, the registered owner(s) must file, no matter who was driving the car.

Who is sued?

It is said that you can sue anybody for anything. But suing the correct party is important. Here are some general guidelines:

- Name the individual you are suing with the most complete name you have for that person.

- If you are suing an individually owned business, list the name of the owner and the business.

- If it is a partnership, list the names of all partners, even if your dispute is only with one of them.

- If you are suing a corporation, list its full name. Usually the owners of a corporation are not legally responsible for the debts of

note If you are suing more than one person on a claim arising from the same incident, each defendant must be listed and served separately. Even married couples must be listed by their individual names.

the corporation, so they shouldn't be sued unless you have a personal claim against them that is separate from their role as owners of the corporation.

- If your claim arises from a motor vehicle accident, list both the driver and the registered owner (if they are different). This information is available at the time of the accident, from the state Department of Motor Vehicles, or from the local police department.

Before suing a business, make sure you are suing the true owner. A judgment against an incorrect owner is worthless. To verify your information, check the county clerk's office, the state agency for fictitious name records, or the city or county business tax and license office for a list of business owners paying taxes. If the business you are suing is likely to be registered with a state agency, check the phone book for a public information number for state offices.

note

If you sue a minor, list both the minor's name and the legal guardian. Minors can't usually be held responsible for breach of contract. A guardian is only responsible if the child is guilty of malicious misconduct or causes damage in an auto accident after getting parental permission to drive. Check local laws before suing a minor.

If you are suing a person's estate, your claim must be made in writing to the executor, administrator or personal representative of the estate. If there is no probate proceeding, you can sue the heirs directly.

Different rules govern a suit against a government agency. You must file a claim with the agency within six months of the incident and have it denied in writing. When you have a letter of denial from the agency, then you can file in Small Claims Court. Suits against the federal government or its agencies must be brought in Federal District Court, not Small Claims Court.

Where to sue

Almost without exception, the suit must be filed where the defendant lives. Check local laws. If the dispute occurred some distance from where you live, check the local laws there, as requirements may vary. They may require the claim be filed where the defendant lives or has a business, where the accident occurred, where the contract was signed, where the contract was broken, or where the merchandise was purchased.

When checking local laws, note how the jurisdiction is divided—by precincts, cities, counties, or districts. Then note which court falls in the appropriate territory; you may have a choice of courts in which to file your case. Choose the jurisdiction most convenient to you, or the one allowing the highest jurisdictional amount if those amounts vary by jurisdiction.

You cannot force a defendant who lives outside the state in which you bring suit to come to court. If you are suing a corporation incorporated elsewhere that does some business in your state, you can bring suit. If the defendant has no connection to your state, you can only sue by going to his or her jurisdiction.

Filing and serving your lawsuit

5

Chapter 5

Filing and serving your lawsuit

What you'll find in this chapter:

⟶ Types of complaint forms

⟶ Counterclaims

⟶ Continuances

⟶ Service of process (the summons)

⟶ Proof of service

The cost of filing a lawsuit varies (see the Appendix). A plaintiff with a very low income may have the fee waived. The court clerk is required by law to give the plaintiff whatever help he or she needs in filling out the forms, so don't be intimidated by a gruff or indifferent clerk of the court.

Filing a lawsuit requires filling out a Statement of Claim or Complaint that tells the defendant and the court the facts of your dispute. This guide contains nine sample Statements of Claim or Complaints as follows:

1) Account Stated (see the sample on the following page)

2) Open Account

3) For Goods Sold

4) Bad Check

In the <u>County Court</u>

In and for <u>SomeCounty</u> **County,** <u>SomeState</u>

Harry Smith Plaintiff, v. John Doe Defendant.	Case No.: Division: Civil Statement of Claim or Complaint

ACCOUNT STATED

Plaintiff sues Defendant and alleges that:

1. This is an action for damages in the amount of $ 750.00 .

2. This action is brought in a county in which venue is proper.

3. Before the institution of this action, Plaintiff and Defendant had business dealings between them and on September 15, 2010 they agreed to the resulting balance.

4. Plaintiff rendered a statement to Defendant, a copy being attached as Exhibit "A," and Defendant did not object.

5. Defendant owes Plaintiff $ 750.00 that is due with interest.

Wherefore, Plaintiff demands judgment for damages in the amount of

$ 750.00 plus interest and costs.

By: *Harry Smith*
_____
Signature

Harry Smith
_____
Print Name

Address: 81 Oak Street
_____

SomeCity, SomeState 99999
_____

Phone: (123) 456-7890

5) Promissory Note

6) For Conversion of Property

7) For Money Lent

8) For Defective Property

9) For Damages

Each is self-explanatory. If the claim is based on a contract, attach a copy of the contract to your Statement of Claim. Save the details for your day in court.

What happens when you file

When you file, the clerk gives your Statement of Claim a case number and a court date. You, the defendant and judge each get a copy. Some states require that the defendant respond in writing or fill out a form. Most states simply require that the defendant appear in court at the appointed time. You can obtain a copy of the procedures for your Small Claims Court from the court clerk.

DEFINITION

A defendant having a claim against the plaintiff arising from the same incident may file a *counterclaim*. (If the claim arises from a different incident, the defendant must file an independent lawsuit, in which he or she becomes the plaintiff.) A counterclaim must be filed in the clerk's office of the appropriate jurisdiction within a certain time limit (check local laws). It must be served on the plaintiff and heard at the same time the plaintiff's case is heard.

If either party needs to postpone, or "continue," the court date, that party should call the other party and arrange a mutually convenient new time. Notify the clerk of the new court date in a letter signed by both parties. If the parties cannot agree, the party who wants the change must notify the clerk. Court correspondence should include the case number, plaintiff's name, current court date, a request for a continuance, the circumstances that make it impossible for the party to attend, and a statement that the other party is unwilling to agree to a new court date. Keep a copy of all correspondence.

Service of process

DEFINITION

Delivering the plaintiff's Statement of Claim and a Summons, or notice, to the defendant is called *service of process*. Each person named in your suit must be served, or notified, individually. In some states, where a defendant is served is important. Check the regulations governing service in your state.

The form a Summons takes can also vary from state to state. A sample Summons is included in this guide for your review, but be sure to ask the clerk of the Small Claims Court where you file your suit to provide you with a valid Summons for that jurisdiction.

A sample Summons follows.

In the <u>County Court</u>

In and for <u>SomeCounty</u> **County,** <u>SomeState</u>

Harry Smith	Case No.:
	Division: Civil
Plaintiff,	
v.	
John Doe	
Defendant.	

SUMMONS

STATE OF SomeState

To All and Singular Sheriffs of the State:

You are hereby commanded to serve this summons and a copy of the complaint or petition in this action upon Defendant:

John Doe, 10 Main Street, SomeCity, SomeState 99999

By Serving:

John Doe

The Defendant is required to serve written defenses to the complaint or petition on Plaintiff at:

81 Oak Street, SomeCity, SomeState 99999

within twenty (20) days after service of this summons on the Defendant, exclusive of the date of service, and to file the original of the defenses with the Clerk of this Court either before service on Plaintiff or immediately thereafter. If the Defendant fails to do so, a default will be entered against the Defendant for the relief demanded in the complaint or petition.

Witness my hand and the seal of said court this 7th day of May , 2010 .

Harriet Clerk
_____
Clerk of the County Court

By: *Jane Clerk*
_____
Deputy Clerk

Serving the summons

The fees charged for service of process are in addition to filing fees, and may vary from state to state. There are three methods of serving a summons:

1) *Certified or registered mail* is the easiest and least expensive method and is allowed in most states. If the defendant refuses to sign for the summons, it must be delivered in a more expensive way.

2) *A professional process server* is required in some states. The server may be a sheriff, who charges about $30 for this service, or it can be someone who makes a living serving summonses. Check with the clerk's office for a reputable private process server. In some jurisdictions you must file a motion to use such a service.

note

If the defendant cannot be located in two or three attempts, you will be billed for attempted service. Then you must determine the best time and place for service and obtain an alias summons, or a copy of the original summons, from the clerk's office at an additional fee, in order to try again.

3) *A non-professional server* is permitted to serve a summons in some states, in which case you can ask a friend who is not part of the claim to serve for free.

While a private business person can be quicker and less expensive, a uniformed officer appearing at the defendant's home or work could be worth the extra cost, as it underscores the seriousness of the claim.

A sample Proof of Service follows.

In the <u>County Court</u>

In and for <u>SomeCounty</u> County, <u>SomeState</u>

	Case No.:
Harry Smith	Division: Civil
Plaintiff,	
v.	
John Doe	
Defendant.	

PROOF OF SERVICE

State of <u>SomeState</u>
County of <u>SomeCounty</u> }

I, <u>Joe Process Server</u>, being duly sworn, depose and say, I am over 18 years of age and not a party to this action. On <u>November 15, 2010</u>, at <u>2 p.m.</u>, in the County of <u>SomeCounty</u>, City of <u>SomeCity</u>, State of <u>SomeState</u>, I served the Notice of Claim herein on <u>John Doe</u>, known to be the defendant mentioned and described as defendant therein, by delivering the said notice to and leaving the same with known to me to be the <u>President</u> of the said defendant corporation.

<u>*Joe Process Server*</u>
Process Server

On <u>November 16, 2010</u>, before me, <u>Nick Notary</u>, personally appeared <u>Joe Process Server</u>, personally known to me (or proved to me on the basis of satisfactory evidence) to be the person(s) whose name(s) is/are subscribed to the within instrument and acknowledged to me that he/she/they executed the same in his/her/their authorized capacity(ies), and that by his/her/their signature(s) on the instrument the person(s), or the entity upon behalf of which the person(s) acted, executed the instrument.
Witness my hand and official seal.

Signature <u>*Nick Notary*</u>
My commission expires: <u>12/31/11</u>

Affiant ____ Known ✔ Produced ID
Type of ID <u>State Driver's License</u>
(Seal)

If you are suing the partner or sole proprietor in a business, he or she must be served individually. If you are suing a corporation, an officer must be served. If you are serving a public agency, call the government body in question and ask who should be served.

 The plaintiff files a Proof of Service or affidavit in the clerk's office after a summons has been successfully served. The clerk can provide the form and more information.

All states require that a summons be served within a certain time prior to the trial. Check the requirements in your state. If you fail to notify the defendant in that time, request a new court date and serve the summons again.

An improperly served defendant should appear in court if they are able, whether or not they were served properly. If a defendant is improperly served and unable to appear, he or she should notify the clerk's office and request a continuance to a more convenient time. If compromise seems like a good idea as the court date looms, put it in writing and get a signed statement from the plaintiff that the lawsuit will be forever dropped. The Covenant Not to Sue is ideal for this.

note Even if service of process isn't timely, a judge may issue a default judgment against a defendant who does not appear in court.

Preparing your case

Chapter 6

Preparing your case

No matter what kind of case you have, you will want to gather as much evidence as possible to support it. That evidence will include any written documents—whether a napkin, the back of a placemat or a signed contract; witnesses to the agreement, dispute or accident; and any expert testimony you can produce.

> Remember, if you don't understand your case, you can't expect the judge to understand it. So do your homework!

Absent a contract, bill or repair order, a witness helps substantiate your claim. But if you don't have any of the above, the next best thing is to document the incident or dispute in a letter to your adversary.

Don't expect to win your case solely on the fact that your car worked before you took it in for repair and now it doesn't. Be prepared to explain exactly what doesn't work and why. Get an expert to testify for you in this area if you have to.

Property damage

In a property damage suit, use the complaint For Damages to briefly state your claim. Then begin gathering evidence to back up your claim. Bring before and after pictures if you have them. Obtain several repair estimates. If repairing the item isn't going to return it to its original condition, get an expert to testify to that fact. Obtain written appraisals of the item's value to document your loss. Have witnesses testify to the item's appearance before the damage occurred.

Harry took his tweed jacket to be dry-cleaned at ABC Cleaners, where he regularly had his shirts cleaned and pressed. Harry had worn the 6-month-old jacket only three times. It had never been cleaned. When Harry dropped off the jacket at ABC on Tuesday, he could have easily worn it two or three more times before having it cleaned, but he wanted to look especially nice for his first date with Mildred. On Friday, Harry picked up his $250 jacket and couldn't believe its condition. There were spots on the lapel and it had shrunk at least half a size.

> HINT)) The more evidence you have to support how the property appeared before the damage, the better.

Harry was hopping mad. He expected ABC's owner, Joe, to accept responsibility and pay for the damaged jacket. But Joe refused, saying the jacket was stained when Harry brought it in and that his cleaning process is 100 percent guaranteed not to shrink.

Of course, Harry knew differently and began to gather his evidence. He dug out the receipt from the clothier who custom-tailored the jacket for Harry six months earlier. The receipt included the measurements for the shoulders and arms. He talked with Sarah, who saw Harry wearing the jacket the night before he took it to the cleaners. Sarah could testify about the stainless jacket's fit. Harry also had a picture of himself wearing the jacket about a month before he had it cleaned.

The receipt, the picture, Sarah's testimony and the testimony of the tailor gave Harry a pretty strong case against Joe, who wasn't even at the cleaners when Harry dropped off the jacket. Since Joe owns the business, he would be liable for any damages, whether they were caused by him or one of his employees.

Personal injury

Many personal injury cases have the ingredients for big payouts, in which case it is a good idea to consult an attorney before proceeding on your own. Let's take the case of Raquel, a 20-year-old Florida college student who was recently injured through no fault of her own.

Raquel was watching the raucous dancing at a club near the local university when all of a sudden she found herself spinning in the air above the heads of three burly young men caught up in the club's atmosphere. The next minute, Raquel was staring at six Reebok-clad feet and rubbing her bruised and aching hip. Raquel didn't think she was hurt at the

> **note**
> Remember the ingredients every case must have—damage or injury, negligence or intent to do harm, and loss of money or property.

time, but the next day she could hardly move from her bed. She ended up in the hospital for two days with a fractured hip, and had to drop several of her classes.

Does Raquel have a case? You bet! Raquel was definitely injured by the negligence of the three men. She has hospital reports and bills to prove it. She definitely lost money, not only in the medical expenses she incurred but also in the wasted tuition for classes she couldn't finish. But there's more to this case than what you see on the surface.

The injuries Raquel suffered will produce long-term, lasting effects, something Raquel should consider when filing her suit, so she can recover for future medical costs associated with the chronic pain and suffering caused by her injury. Once Raquel considers those issues, her case becomes a true civil matter and, as with most personal injury cases these days, no longer suitable for Small Claims Court.

note

On occasion, however, minor personal injury cases, often involving animals, do make it to Small Claims Court. Here again, use the statement of claim For Damages to briefly outline the reason for your complaint. Then gather the evidence to support it.

Contract disputes

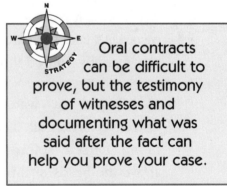

Oral contracts can be difficult to prove, but the testimony of witnesses and documenting what was said after the fact can help you prove your case.

Depending on the specifics of the case, any one of several complaint forms can be used for a contract dispute, including Account Stated, Open Account, Promissory Note, For Goods Sold, For Damages, or For Money Lent. Preparing for court can be easy if your contract is in writing. Be sure to bring a copy of the contract to court with you.

Alison called Shirley about an apartment Shirley had for rent. After looking at the apartment, Alison gave Shirley a $500 deposit and left, expecting to move into her new home the first of the month. Alison gave notice to her present landlord, notified the utilities of her change of address and hired a mover. Two weeks later, Shirley rented the apartment to someone else. Although Shirley returned Alison's deposit, Alison is still out money she paid to the mover and her present landlord for breaking her lease.

There was no written contract here, but it was implied by Shirley's acceptance of the $500 deposit that she would rent the apartment to Alison. When Shirley rented the apartment to someone else, the contract was breached. Here, all Alison needs is evidence of the payment of the deposit—a canceled check, a withdrawal slip, a witness to the transaction. If she paid Shirley in cash, then Alison should write a letter to Shirley outlining the facts of the incident as she best remembers them. This letter and any response from Shirley could then be used as evidence that a contract existed.

A sample complaint For Damages follows.

In the County Court

In and for SomeCounty **County,** SomeState

Alison Doe Plaintiff, v. Shirley Smith Defendant.	Case No.: Division: Civil Complaint

FOR DAMAGES

Plaintiff, Alison Doe , sues defendant, Shirley Smith, and alleges:

1. This is an action for damages which are less than $ 1,000 .

2. Defendant owes Plaintiff $ 690.00 that are due with interest since June 10 , 2010 .

3. Defendant is obligated to pay to Plaintiff the sum of $ 690.00 because Defendant breached oral contract to rent vacant apartment to plaintiff who had paid security deposit to Defendant for the same .

WHEREFORE plaintiff demands judgment for damages against defendant in the amount of $ 690.00 , plus prejudgment interest and court costs.

By: *Alison Doe*
Signature

By: Alison Doe
Print Name

Address: 14 Oak Street #1

SomeCity, SomeState 99999

Phone: (123) 456-7890

Defective product

Injuries resulting from the use of a defective product, whether a can opener, curling iron, electric tooth brush or razor, require no proof of negligence to recover damages from the manufacturer.

Harry bought a pull-start lawn mower. When he tried to start it, the cord snapped and hit him in the face. Harry sued the manufacturer and recovered $1,500 in damages as a result of the injuries he suffered from the use of the defective lawn mower.

This guide contains a complaint specifically for defective product cases. A sample complaint For Defective Product follows.

note

While most defective product cases end up in formal court, those small enough to be heard in Small Claims Court need only concern themselves with proving that the injury resulted from using the defective product.

In the <u>County Court</u>

In and for <u>SomeCounty</u> **County,** <u>SomeState</u>

Harry Anderson Plaintiff, v. Lawn Mowers, Inc. Defendant.	Case No.: Division: Civil Complaint

FOR DEFECTIVE PRODUCT

Plaintiff, <u>Harry Anderson</u>, sues defendant, <u>Lawn Mowers, Inc.</u>, and alleges:

1. This is an action for damages which are less than $ <u>2,000.00</u>.

2. Defendant manufactured a product known and described as (describe product): <u>a pull-start lawn mower, model B250</u>

3. Defendant warranted that the product was reasonably fit for its intended use as (describe intended use): <u>a pull-start lawn mower</u>

4. On <u>February 18</u>, <u>2010</u>, at <u>2:26 p.m.</u> in <u>SomeCounty</u> County, State of <u>SomeState</u>, <u>the product malfunctioned, causing head injury to the plaintiff. The pull-start cord snapped off, hitting plaintiff in the face.</u> (describe the occurrence and defect that resulted in injury) while being used for its intended purpose causing injuries to plaintiff who was then a user of the product.

5. As a result plaintiff was injured in and against his/her body and extremities, suffered pain therefrom, incurred medical expenses in the treatment of the injuries, and suffered physical handicap, and his/her working ability was impaired; the injuries are either permanent or continuing in their nature and plaintiff will suffer the losses and impairment in the future.

WHEREFORE plaintiff demands judgment for damages against defendant in the amount of $<u>2,000.00</u>, plus prejudgment interest and court costs.

By: *Harry Anderson*
<u>Signature</u>
By: <u>Harry Anderson</u>
<u>Print Name</u>
Address: <u>444 Green Street</u>

<u>SomeCity, SomeState 99999</u>

Phone: <u>(123) 456-7890</u>

Breach of warranty

Unlike product liability, breach of warranty cases require a contract between the manufacturer or seller and the buyer. But the buyer need not prove negligence to recover damages. If a warranty comes with a product you purchase and the product breaks down within the warranty period, you should get your money back. To recover, be sure you have a copy of the contract and the warranty.

Document your attempts to settle the dispute and keep copies of your correspondence to present in court in the event your settlement attempt fails. A complaint For Damages can be used to state your claim in breach of warranty cases.

> Remember, give the seller ample opportunity to fix or replace the product (usually thirty days) before filing suit.

Consumer violations

Your state statutes are full of laws that protect you as a consumer. Chief among these state consumer protection laws is the *Uniform Commercial Code*. You can probably find the law you're looking for in the state statutes or codes, located in your local law library in or near the courthouse. When one of these laws is broken, you need only cite the statute or code to the judge to recover damages caused by a violation of a consumer protection law.

Neighborly disputes

Being neighborly can sometimes cost you, especially when a neighbor takes advantage of your generosity. Fortunately, you have two remedies: complaints For Conversion of Property and For Money Lent.

If Joe borrowed your 100-piece tool set six months ago and now refuses to give it back, take him to court. If John borrowed $500 from you three months ago and has yet to repay you, take him to court. In both cases, however, the more evidence you have to support your claim, the more likely you are to win. So document the circumstances behind your claim.

A sample complaint For Conversion of Property is on the following page.

Should you hire an attorney?

Remember, you can usually hire an attorney to represent you, but think twice about doing so. Even if your state allows representation and your opponent uses a lawyer, it's probably unnecessary and expensive. You may want to consult an attorney about the laws applicable to your case, rather than having one represent you. This is a less expensive way to arm yourself with legal knowledge for your 15 minutes in court.

As the unrepresented party you may even enjoy a perceived advantage with the judge.

In the County Court

In and for SomeCounty **County,** SomeState

Case No.:
Division: Civil

Harry Handy

Plaintiff,
v.

Complaint

Frank Fixit
Defendant.

FOR CONVERSION OF PROPERTY

Plaintiff, Harry Handy , sues defendant,
Frank Fixit , and alleges:

1.   This is an action for damages which are less than $ 2,000 .

2.   On or about July 12 , 2010 , defendant converted
      to his/her own use Plaintiff's 100-piece tool set
      (insert description of property converted) that was then the property of
      plaintiff of the value of $ 650.00 .

WHEREFORE plaintiff demands judgment for damages against defendant in
the amount of $ 650.00 , plus prejudgment interest and court costs.

By: *Harry Handy*
    Signature
By: Harry Handy
    Print Name
Address: 99 Lake Road

SomeCity, SomeState 99999

Phone: (123) 456-7890

Going to court

Chapter 7

Going to court

What you'll find in this chapter:

➡️ Collecting by wage garnishment

➡️ Using depositions to discover assets

➡️ Using the Rule to Show Cause

➡️ Attaching personal property

➡️ Liens and bench warrants

Your day in court

On the day of your hearing, get to court on time. A case is normally decided in favor of the party who appears, so it is important to be in court on the date and at the time your hearing is scheduled.

If you're the defendant, don't just decide not to show up. By appearing before the judge you can fight the claim or at least explain that you can't afford to pay it and want more time.

If the plaintiff fails to appear, the judge may decide in favor of the defendant, or may dismiss the case. If the case is dismissed, the plaintiff may immediately move to have the order dismissing the case vacated, or canceled, so the defendant must respond to the complaint. If neither party appears, the judge may take the case off the calendar, in which case the plaintiff can refile. A sample Motion to Vacate Dismissal follows.

In the <u>County Court</u>

In and for <u>SomeCounty</u> **County,** <u>SomeState</u>

Alison Doe

Plaintiff,

v.

Shirley Smith

Defendant.

Case No.:
Division: Civil

MOTION TO VACATE DISMISSAL

This cause having come to be heard on July 15, 2010
and the court having heard argument and being otherwise fully advised in the premises it is upon consideration thereof ordered and adjudged that:

1.   The motion is to vacate the judge's ruling to dismiss the case.

2.   A hearing is set for August 15, 2010 to allow
plaintiff to present her case.

Done and ordered on   August 1 , 2010 in chambers in
County Court   , SomeCounty   County, SomeState   .

Henry Honor
Judge

Copies Furnished:
Alison Doe
Shirley Smith

If you are the defendant, make sure you know where the courthouse is (the plaintiff has probably been there several times to file). Both the defendant and the plaintiff need to be sure that any witnesses know where and when to show up.

E-Z Tip
To feel and look prepared, arrive at the courthouse a few minutes early. Wear conservative, professional-looking clothing.

If the courtroom is full of plaintiffs and defendants, you can watch other small claims cases being heard. Pay attention, as their actions will help you know what you should do when your case is called.

Even in the courthouse, it is not too late to settle the case if both parties can come to an agreement. If not, the judge may hear the case immediately or turn it over for trial, meaning you will have to return another day. You can usually learn ahead of time how cases are typically disposed of in your court. In larger jurisdictions be prepared to return for trial. Most first appearances only give the defendant the opportunity to admit or deny the charges; the merits of the case are heard at a later date.

If your case is heard immediately, both you and the defendant will state your case. The judge may ask a few questions and make a decision, or the final judgment may not be issued for a few days.

If you win: collecting

If the judgment is in the plaintiff's favor, there's no guarantee that an uncooperative defendant will docilely write you a check because you've won. Your recourse then is to obtain a *Writ of Execution*. The laws governing this recourse vary by state. The following methods are typical:

Garnishments

DEFINITION

States allow wages or property to be *garnished*, or attached, to satisfy certain debts. The garnishment is in effect until the debt is paid. This can be done by notifying the debtor's employer to withhold a state-specified amount from the debtor's salary, or by notifying the debtor's bank to put a hold on any funds in the debtor's name. Forms need to be filed with the circuit court clerk, who can tell you what forms to use, who must fill them out, and how much the filing fee is. Filing fees can usually be billed to the debtor.

Depositions

If you are not aware of the debtor's assets, the debtor can be required to produce records that provide information on the debtor's employment, real estate and other property and financial records so you may garnish assets to satisfy the debt. In some states, you can have the defendant questioned by the court as to the assets the defendant owns. Some courts will automatically send the defendant a Notice of Taking Deposition.

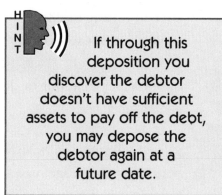

HINT

If through this deposition you discover the debtor doesn't have sufficient assets to pay off the debt, you may depose the debtor again at a future date.

For those that don't, a sample Notice of Taking Deposition follows.

In the _County Court_

In and for _SomeCounty_ **County,** _SomeState_

Alison Doe Plaintiff, v. Shirley Smith Defendant.	Case No.: Division: Civil

NOTICE OF TAKING DEPOSITION

To: Shirley Smith
       18 Elm Street
       SomeCity, SomeState 99999

   You are hereby notified that before a person authorized by law to take depositions, Plaintiff will take the deposition of Shirley Smith   by oral examination for the purpose of discovery or for such other purposes as are permitted under applicable rules of procedure. Said deposition will be taken at 15 Justice Avenue, SomeCity, SomeState on:

   Date: August 31, 2010   Time: 9:00 a.m.

The oral examination will continue from day to day until completed.

   I hereby certify that a true and correct copy of this Notice of Deposition was furnished by mail on July 31, 2010   to the parties indicated above.

Harriet Clerk
Clerk of the County Court

By: _Jane Clerk_
Deputy Clerk

Rule to Show Cause

DEFINITION

If the first two methods of arranging payment fail, you may have a *Rule to Show Cause*, or *Motion for Contempt*, served on the debtor, which requires the debtor to explain the reason for non-payment to a judge.

Attachment of personal property

If the debtor has business assets, a boat, jewelry, stocks or other assets, you may take the proceeds from the court-ordered sale of such property. If the debtor has not responded to a deposition to reveal the necessary information, it is up to the plaintiff to know or learn what property is available, what its value is and where it is.

To attach personal property, very detailed forms must be filed and fees paid, so contact your clerk's office.

Liens on real property

You can put a claim, or "lien," on the debtor's property, which allows you to collect your money when the property is sold. There can be more than one lien on a property, each having its own priority when the property is liquidated.

Bench warrants

If all else fails, a bench warrant can be issued calling for the debtor's arrest. The debtor must then pay his debt, as well as other costs, to get out of jail.

The decision is yours

Is your case a good one for Small Claims Court? Only you can decide.

Choosing to go to Small Claims Court can be difficult, time-consuming and frustrating. But you'll be better prepared after reading this guide. You'll know if you have a case and, what's more, whether you have a winning case. You'll know what facts, documents and testimony to gather before you go into court, and you'll know when and when not to seek the advice or aid of an attorney. Good luck!

The forms in this guide

> **NOTE: The forms in this publication have been reduced in size. To restore them to their correct size on a photocopier, increase the size to 122% .**

About These Made E-Z Forms:
While the legal forms and documents in this product generally conform to the requirements of courts nationwide, certain courts may have additional requirements. Before completing and filing the forms in this product, check with the clerk of the court concerning these requirements.

In the _____

In and for _____ **County,** _____

	Case No.:
	Division: Civil
Plaintiff,	
v.	
Defendant.	

STIPULATION OF SETTLEMENT

The plaintiff, _____, and the defendant, _____,
hereby agree that this claim is settled for the sum of $ _____, to be paid on or before
_____ to plaintiff at

or as follows:

Upon payment, Plaintiff and Defendant shall be released from any liability relating to this dispute.

Plaintiff is entitled to judgment without further notice in the event of default in payment by defendant.

Dated:

_____
Plaintiff

_____
Defendant

In the _____

In and for _____ County, _____

Plaintiff,	Case No.:
v.	Division: Civil
Defendant.	

SUMMONS

STATE OF

To All and Singular Sheriffs of the State:

You are hereby commanded to serve this summons and a copy of the complaint or petition in this action upon Defendant:

By Serving:

The Defendant is required to serve written defenses to the complaint or petition on Plaintiff at:

within twenty (20) days after service of this summons on the Defendant, exclusive of the date of service, and to file the original of the defenses with the Clerk of this Court either before service on Plaintiff or immediately thereafter. If the Defendant fails to do so, a default will be entered against the Defendant for the relief demanded in the complaint or petition.

Witness my hand and the seal of said court this   day of   ,   .

_____

Clerk of the County Court

By:_____

Deputy Clerk

In the _____

In and for _____ **County,** _____

	Case No.:
	Division: Civil
Plaintiff,	
v.	
	Statement of Claim
	or Complaint
Defendant.	

ACCOUNT STATED

Plaintiff sues Defendant and alleges that:

1.   This is an action for damages in the amount of $.

2.   This action is brought in a county in which venue is proper.

3.   Before the institution of this action, Plaintiff and Defendant had business dealings between them and on   they agreed to the resulting balance.

4.   Plaintiff rendered a statement to Defendant, a copy being attached as Exhibit "A," and Defendant did not object.

5.   Defendant owes Plaintiff $ that is due with interest.

Wherefore, Plaintiff demands judgment for damages in the amount of $ plus interest and costs.

By: _____
Signature of Plaintiff

_____
Print Name

Address: _____

_____

Phone: _____

In the _____

In and for _____ County, _____

Plaintiff, v. Defendant.	Case No.: Division: Civil Statement of Claim or Complaint

OPEN ACCOUNT

Plaintiff sues Defendant and alleges that:

1.   This is an action for damages in the amount of $.

2.   Defendant owes Plaintiff $ that is due with interest on open account according to Exhibit "A."

Wherefore, Plaintiff demands judgment for damages on the amount of $ plus interest and costs.

By: _____
  Signature of Plaintiff

  _____
  Print Name

Address: _____

  _____

  Phone: _____

In the _____

In and for _____ County, _____

Plaintiff,

v.

Defendant.

Case No.:
Division: Civil

Statement of Claim
or Complaint

FOR GOODS SOLD

Plaintiff sues Defendant and alleges that:

1.   This is an action for damages in the amount of $.

2.   Defendant owes Plaintiff $ that is due with interest, for goods sold and delivered and/or services rendered by Plaintiff to Defendant, as detailed in Exhibit "A."

Wherefore, Plaintiff demands judgment for damages in the amount of $ plus interest and costs.

By: _____
Signature of Plaintiff

_____
Print Name

Address: _____

_____

Phone: _____

In the _____

In and for _____ County, _____

Plaintiff,

v.

Defendant.

Case No.:
Division: Civil

Statement of Claim
or Complaint

BAD CHECK

Plaintiff sues Defendant and alleges that:

1.   This is an action for damages in the amount of $_____ (total amount due).

2.   On _____ Defendant executed a check in the amount of $_____ , payable to Plaintiff and delivered it to Plaintiff. A copy of the check is attached hereto.

3.   The check was presented for payment to the drawee bank but payment was refused.

4.   Plaintiff holds the check and it has not been paid.

5.   Defendant owes Plaintiff $_____ that is due with interest.

6.   Plaintiff made written demand for payment of the check upon Defendant pursuant to statutes but payment has not been made.

7.   Pursuant to statutes, Defendant is liable to Plaintiff for: (a) the amount of the check; (b) a service charge equal to 5% of the amount of the check; and, (c) additional damages equal to triple the amount of the check.

Wherefore, Plaintiff demands judgment for actual damages in the amount of $_____ plus the statutory 5% service charge plus statutory treble damages plus interest, costs and attorney's fees.

By: _____
Signature of Plaintiff

_____
Print Name

Address: _____

_____

Phone: _____

87

In the _____

In and for _____ County, _____

Plaintiff, v. Defendant.	Case No.: Division: Civil

MOTION TO VACATE DISMISSAL

    This cause having come to be heard on _____ and the court having heard argument and being otherwise fully advised in the premises it is upon consideration thereof ordered and adjudged that:

1.   The motion is to vacate the judge's ruling to dismiss the case.

2.

    Done and ordered on _____ in chambers in _____ County, _____ .

_____
Judge

Copies Furnished:

In the _____

In and for _____ **County,** _____

Plaintiff, v. Defendant.	Case No.: Division: Civil Statement of Claim or Complaint

PROMISSORY NOTE

Plaintiff sues Defendant and alleges that:

1.   This is an action for damages in the amount of $.

2.   On   Defendant executed and delivered a promissory note, a copy being attached, to Plaintiff in   County,   .

3.   Plaintiff owns and holds the note.

4.   Defendant failed to pay

    a)   the note when due.
    b)   the installment payment due on the note on   , and Plaintiff elected to accelerate payment of the balance.

5.   Defendant owes Plaintiff $ that is due with interest on the note since   .

Wherefore, Plaintiff demands judgment for damages against the defendant.

By: _____
        Signature of Plaintiff

_____
Print Name

Address: _____

_____

Phone: _____

Note: A copy of the note must be attached. Use paragraph 4a or 4b as applicable.

COVENANT NOT TO SUE

FOR GOOD AND VALUABLE CONSIDERATION RECEIVED, the undersigned being the holder of an actual, asserted or prospective claim against _____, arising from (describe obligation or claim):

do hereby covenant that I/we shall not commence or maintain any suit thereon against said party, whether at law or in equity, provided nothing in this agreement shall constitute a release of this or any other party thereto.

This covenant shall be binding upon and inure to the benefit of the parties, their successors, assigns and executors, administrators, personal representatives and heirs.

The undersigned affixes and seals this _____ day of _____ , ____ .

Signed in the presence of:

_____   _____
Witness   Obligor

State of
County of

On _____ , before me, _____ ,
personally appeared _____ ,
personally known to me (or proved to me on the basis of satisfactory evidence) to be the person(s) whose name(s) is/are subscribed to the within instrument and acknowledged to me that he/she/they executed the same in his/her/their authorized capacity(ies), and that by his/her/their signature(s) on the instrument the person(s), or the entity upon behalf of which the person(s) acted, executed the instrument.
Witness my hand and official seal.

Signature_____

My commission expires: _____   Affiant _____ Known _____ Produced ID
                                        Type of ID _____
                                                              (Seal)

In the _____

In and for _____ **County,** _____

Plaintiff,

v.

Defendant.

Case No.:
Division: Civil

NOTICE OF TAKING DEPOSITION

To:

     You are hereby notified that before a person authorized by law to take depositions, Plaintiff will take the deposition of _____ by oral examination for the purpose of discovery or for such other purposes as are permitted under applicable rules of procedure. Said deposition will be taken at
on:

Date: Time:

The oral examination will continue from day to day until completed.

     I hereby certify that a true and correct copy of this Notice of Deposition was furnished by mail on _____ to the parties indicated above.

_____

Clerk of the County Court

By: _____

Deputy Clerk

In the _____

In and for _____ County, _____

Case No.:

Division: Civil

Plaintiff,

v.

Complaint

_____ Defendant.

FOR MONEY LENT

Plaintiff, _____, sues defendant, _____, and alleges:

1.   This is an action for damages which are less than $_____.

2.   Defendant owes plaintiff $_____ that is due with interest since _____, _____, for money lent by plaintiff to defendant on _____, _____.

WHEREFORE plaintiff demands judgment for damages against defendant in the amount of $_____, plus prejudgment interest and court costs.

By: _____
Signature of Plaintiff

_____
Print name

Address: _____

_____

Phone: _____

In the _____
In and for _____ County, _____

Plaintiff, v.	Case No.: Division: Civil Complaint
_____ Defendant.	

FOR CONVERSION OF PROPERTY

Plaintiff, _____, sues defendant, _____, and alleges:

1. This is an action for damages which are less than $_____.

2. On or about _____, _____, defendant converted to his/her own use _____ (insert description of property converted) that was then the property of plaintiff of the value of $_____.

WHEREFORE plaintiff demands judgment for damages against defendant in the amount of $_____, plus prejudgment interest and court costs.

By: _____
Signature of Plaintiff

_____
Print name

Address: _____

_____

Phone: _____

In the _____

In and for _____ **County,** _____

	Case No.:
	Division: Civil
Plaintiff,	
v.	Complaint
Defendant.	

FOR DAMAGES

Plaintiff, _____, sues defendant, _____, and alleges:

1.   This is an action for damages which are less than $_____.

2.   Defendant owes Plaintiff $_____ that are due with interest since _____, _____.

3.   Defendant is obligated to pay to Plaintiff the sum of $_____ because_____.

WHEREFORE plaintiff demands judgment for damages against defendant in the amount of $_____, plus prejudgment interest and court costs.

By: _____
Signature of Plaintiff

_____
Print Name

Address: _____

_____

Phone: _____

In the _____

In and for _____ **County,** _____

Plaintiff, v. _____ Defendant.	Case No.: Division: Civil Complaint

FOR DEFECTIVE PRODUCT

Plaintiff, _____, sues defendant, _____, and alleges:

1.   This is an action for damages which are less than $_____.

2.   Defendant manufactured a product known and described as (describe product):

3.   Defendant warranted that the product was reasonably fit for its intended use as (describe intended use):

4.   On _____, _____, at _____ in _____ County, State of _____, the product _____ (describe the occurrence and defect that resulted in injury) while being used for its intended purpose causing injuries to plaintiff who was then a user of the product.

5.   As a result plaintiff was injured in and against his/her body and extremities, suffered pain therefrom, incurred medical expenses in the treatment of the injuries, and suffered physical handicap, and his/her working ability was impaired; the injuries are either permanent or continuing in their nature and plaintiff will suffer the losses and impairment in the future.

WHEREFORE plaintiff demands judgment for damages against defendant in the amount of $_____, plus prejudgment interest and court costs.

By: _____

Address: _____

_____

Phone: _____

In the _____

In and for _____ County, _____

Plaintiff, v. Defendant.	Case No.: Division: Civil

PROOF OF SERVICE

State of
County of   }

I, _____, being duly sworn, depose and say, I am over 18 years of age and not a party to this action. On _____, at _____, in the County of _____, City of _____, State of _____, I served the Notice of Claim herein on _____, known to be the defendant mentioned and described as defendant therein, by delivering the said notice to and leaving the same with known to me to be the _____ of the said defendant corporation.

_____
Process Server

On _____, before me, _____, personally appeared _____, personally known to me (or proved to me on the basis of satisfactory evidence) to be the person(s) whose name(s) is/are subscribed to the within instrument and acknowledged to me that he/she/they executed the same in his/her/their authorized capacity(ies), and that by his/her/their signature(s) on the instrument the person(s), or the entity upon behalf of which the person(s) acted, executed the instrument.
Witness my hand and official seal.
Signature_____

My commission expires: _____   Affiant ____ Known ___ Produced ID
Type of ID _____
(Seal)

Glossary of useful terms

A-C

Appeal

The right of a party in a suit to challenge the ruling of the court.

Arbitration

The hearing of a dispute by a disinterested third party appointed by the court.

Assignee

The term applied to a collection agency that represents the plaintiff in Small Claims Court.

Calendar

The schedule of cases to be heard by a particular judge.

Causation

Responsibility and legal accountability for another's loss.

Civil code

Laws governing a state or municipality.

Claim of defendant

Similar to counterclaim, in which the defendant claims the plaintiff owes him or her money.

C-E

Claim of exemption

A debtor claims certain property owned is exempt from attachment to satisfy a debt.

Continuance

Rescheduling, postponing or delaying a court date.

Contract

An agreement between two parties in which one agrees to do something for the other in exchange for something else.

Counterclaim

A suit filed by a defendant against the plaintiff and stemming from the same incident as the plaintiff's claim.

Damages

The dollar amount being sought from a person whose actions have caused an injury or wrong.

Defendant

The person being sued; the debtor.

Dismissal

The ending of a case by order of the judge without either party winning.

Execution on the judgment

Recourse for the winner of a small claims case when the judgment debtor does not pay.

Executor

The personal representative of a person's estate in probate court. Also known as the administrator.

E-L

Express contract

A written agreement; contracts can be express, oral or implied.

Garnish

To place an attachment on wages or income to satisfy a debt.

Guardian ad litem

An adult named guardian of a minor for legal purposes.

Homestead

That part of the equity in a home a debtor can protect from attachment to pay a debt.

Judgment

A ruling by the court.

Jurisdictional limit

The minimum and maximum amounts of money one can sue for in a certain jurisdiction.

Legal theory

A kind of case, or explanation of a case, based on law.

Levy

A way to seize a debtor's money or property for unpaid debts.

Lien

An interest in real estate to recover the payment of a debt.

M-T

Mitigation of damages

n a breach of contract dispute, the plaintiff must take all reasonable steps to limit the amount of damages he or she suffers.

Pain and suffering

The term used to quantify discomfort resulting from a personal injury.

Plaintiff

The person who is suing.

Service of process

The act of notifying the defendant that he or she is being sued.

Statement of claim

A form that begins proceedings in Small Claims Court. Also called a complaint, petition, or plaintiff's claim.

Statute of limitations

The time limit for filing a lawsuit for a certain cause of action in a certain jurisdiction.

Strict liability

Responsibility under the law for a product that malfunctions, with resulting injuries or damage.

Subpoena

A request to appear in court to provide testimony.

Tolled

Suspended; the statute of limitations may be tolled under certain circumstances.

V-W

Venue

The location of a court proceeding.

Wage garnishment

Attachment of wages to satisfy a debt.

Writ of execution

A court order to seize property or money to satisfy a debt.

Resources

••• Online Resources •••

◆ **ADR and Mediation Resources Site**

http://www.adrr.com

◆ **Academy of Family Mediators**

http://www.igc.apc.org/afm

◆ **American Arbitration Association**

http://www.adr.org

◆ **American Bar Association Section of Dispute Resolution**

http://www.abanet.org/dispute

◆ **ConflictNet (Institute for Global Communications)**

http://www.igc.org/igc/conflictnet

◆ **Cornell Legal Information Institute**

http://www.ilr.cornell.edu/depts/ICR

◆ **Courts.Net**

http://www.courts.net/public.html

◆ **HALT**

http://www.halt.org

◆ **Legal.Net**

http://db.legal.net/ldn/welcome/query.cfm

◆ **Legal Information Institute**

http://www.law.cornell.edu/topics/adr.html

◆ **Mediation Information and Resource Center**

http://www.mediate.com

◆ **National Association for Community Mediation (NAFCM)**

http://www.nafcm.org

◆ **People's Court**

http://www.peoplescourt.com

◆ **Virtual Magistrate**

http://vmag.vcilp.org

••• Legal Search Engines •••

◆ **All Law**

http://www.alllaw.com

◆ **American Law Sources On Line**

http://www.lawsource.com/also/searchfm.htm

◆ **Catalaw**

http://www.catalaw.com

◆ **FindLaw**

URL: http://www.findlaw.com

◆ **Hieros Gamos**

http://www.hg.org/hg.html

◆ **InternetOracle**

http://www.internetoracle.com/legal.htm

◆ **LawAid**

http://www.lawaid.com/search.html

◆ **LawCrawler**

http://www.lawcrawler.com

◆ **LawEngine, The**

http://www.fastsearch.com/law

◆ **LawRunner**

http://www.lawrunner.com

◆ **'Lectric Law Library™**

http://www.lectlaw.com

◆ **Legal Search Engines**

http://www.dreamscape.com/frankvad/search.legal.html

◆ **LEXIS/NEXIS Communications Center**

http://www.lexis-nexis.com/lncc/general/search.html

◆ **Meta-Index for U.S. Legal Research**

http://gsulaw.gsu.edu/metaindex

◆ **Seamless Website, The**

http://seamless.com

◆ **USALaw**

http://www.usalaw.com/linksrch.cfm

◆ **WestLaw**

http://westdoc.com   (Registered users only. Fee paid service.)

••• State Bar Associations •••

ALABAMA

Alabama State Bar
415 Dexter Avenue
Montgomery, AL 36104
mailing address:
PO Box 671
Montgomery, AL 36101
(334) 269-1515
http://www.alabar.org

ALASKA

Alaska Bar Association
510 L Street No. 602
Anchorage, AK 99501
mailing address:
PO Box 100279
Anchorage, AK 99510
http://www.alaskabar.org

ARIZONA

State Bar of Arizona
111 West Monroe
Phoenix, AZ 85003-1742
(602) 252-4804
http://www.azbar.org

ARKANSAS

Arkansas Bar Association
400 West Markham
Little Rock, AR 72201
(501) 375-4605
http://www.arkbar.org

CALIFORNIA

State Bar of California
555 Franklin Street
San Francisco, CA 94102
(415) 561-8200
http://www.calbar.org

Alameda County Bar
Association
http://www.acbanet.org

COLORADO

Colorado Bar Association
No. 950, 1900 Grant Street
Denver, CO 80203
(303) 860-1115
http://www.cobar.org

CONNECTICUT

Connecticut Bar Association
101 Corporate Place
Rocky Hill, CT 06067-1894
(203) 721-0025
http://www.ctbar.org

DELAWARE

Delaware State Bar Association
1225 King Street, 10th floor
Wilmington, DE 19801
(302) 658-5279
(302) 658-5278 (lawyer referral
service)
http://www.dsba.org

DISTRICT OF COLUMBIA

District of Columbia Bar
1250 H Street, NW, 6th Floor
Washington, DC 20005
(202) 737-4700

Bar Association of the District
of Columbia
1819 H Street, NW, 12th floor
Washington, DC 20006-3690
(202) 223-6600
http://www.badc.org

FLORIDA

The Florida Bar
The Florida Bar Center
650 Apalachee Parkway
Tallahassee, FL 32399-2300
(850) 561-5600
http://www.flabar.org

GEORGIA

State Bar of Georgia
800 The Hurt Building
50 Hurt Plaza
Atlanta, GA 30303
(404) 527-8700
http://www.gabar.org

HAWAII

Hawaii State Bar Association
1136 Union Mall
Penthouse 1
Honolulu, HI 96813
(808) 537-1868
http://www.hsba.org

IDAHO

Idaho State Bar
PO Box 895
Boise, ID 83701
(208) 334-4500
http://www2.state.id.us/isb

ILLINOIS

Illinois State Bar Association
424 South Second Street
Springfield, IL 62701
(217) 525-1760
http://www.illinoisbar.org

INDIANA

Indiana State Bar Association
230 East Ohio Street
Indianapolis, IN 46204
(317) 639-5465
http://www.ai.org/isba

IOWA

Iowa State Bar Association
521 East Locust
Des Moines, IA 50309
(515) 243-3179
http://www.iowabar.org

KANSAS

Kansas Bar Association
1200 Harrison Street
Topeka, KS 66612-1806
(785) 234-5696
http://www.ksbar.org

KENTUCKY

Kentucky Bar Association
514 West Main Street
Frankfort, KY 40601-1883
(502) 564-3795
http://www.kybar.org

LOUISIANA

Louisiana State Bar Association
601 St. Charles Avenue
New Orleans, LA 70130
(504) 566-1600
http://www.lsba.org

MAINE

Maine State Bar Association
124 State Street
PO Box 788
Augusta, ME 04330
(207) 622-7523

http://www.mainebar.org

MARYLAND

Maryland State Bar Association
520 West Fayette Street
Baltimore, MD 21201
(301) 685-7878

http://www.msba.org/msba

MASSACHUSETTS

Massachusetts Bar Association
20 West Street
Boston, MA 02111
(617) 542-3602
(617) 542-9103 (lawyer referral service)

http://www.massbar.org

MICHIGAN

State Bar of Michigan
306 Townsend Street
Lansing, MI 48933-2083
(517) 372-9030

http://www.michbar.org

MINNESOTA

Minnesota State Bar Association
514 Nicollet Mall
Minneapolis, MN 55402
(612) 333-1183

http://www.mnbar.org

MISSISSIPPI

The Mississippi Bar
643 No. State Street
Jackson, Mississippi 39202
(601) 948-4471

http://www.msbar.org

MISSOURI

The Missouri Bar
P.O. Box 119, 326 Monroe
Jefferson City, Missouri 65102
(314) 635-4128

http://www.mobar.org

MONTANA

State Bar of Montana
46 North Main
PO Box 577
Helena, MT 59624
(406) 442-7660

http://www.montanabar.org

NEBRASKA

Nebraska State Bar Association
635 South 14th Street, 2nd floor
Lincoln, NE 68508
(402) 475-7091

http://www.nebar.com

NEVADA

State Bar of Nevada
201 Las Vegas Blvd.
Las Vegas, NV 89101
(702) 382-2200

http://www.nvbar.org

NEW HAMPSHIRE

New Hampshire Bar
Association
112 Pleasant Street
Concord, NH 03301
(603) 224-6942
http://www.nhbar.org

NEW JERSEY

New Jersey State Bar
Association
One Constitution Square
New Brunswick, NJ 08901-1500
(908) 249-5000

NEW MEXICO

State Bar of New Mexico
5121 Masthead N.E.
Albuquerque, NM 87125
mailing address:
PO Box 25883
Albuquerque, NM 87125
(505) 843-6132
http://www.nmbar.org

NEW YORK

New York State Bar Association
One Elk Street
Albany, NY 12207
(518) 463-3200
http://www.nysba.org

NORTH CAROLINA

North Carolina State Bar
208 Fayetteville Street Mall
Raleigh, NC 27601
mailing address:
PO Box 25908
Raleigh, NC 27611
(919) 828-4620

North Carolina Bar Association
1312 Annapolis Drive
Raleigh, NC 27608
mailing address:
PO Box 3688
Cary, NC 27519-3688
(919) 677-0561
http://www.ncbar.org

NORTH DAKOTA

State Bar Association of North
Dakota
515 1/2 East Broadway, suite 101
Bismarck, ND 58501
mailing address:
PO Box 2136
Bismarck, ND 58502
(701) 255-1404

OHIO

Ohio State Bar Association
1700 Lake Shore Drive
Columbus, OH 43204
mailing address:
PO Box 16562
Columbus, OH 43216-6562
(614) 487-2050
http://www.ohiobar.org

OKLAHOMA

Oklahoma Bar Association
1901 North Lincoln
Oklahoma City, OK 73105
(405) 524-2365
http://www.okbar.org

OREGON

Oregon State Bar
5200 S.W. Meadows Road
PO Box 1689
Lake Oswego, OR 97035-0889
(503) 620-0222
http://www.osbar.org

PENNSYLVANIA

Pennsylvania Bar Association
100 South Street
PO Box 186
Harrisburg, PA 17108
(717) 238-6715
http://www.pabar.org

Pennsylvania Bar Institute
http://www.pbi.org

PUERTO RICO

Puerto Rico Bar Association
PO Box 1900
San Juan, Puerto Rico 00903
(787) 721-3358

RHODE ISLAND

Rhode Island Bar Association
115 Cedar Street
Providence, RI 02903
(401) 421-5740
http://www.ribar.org

SOUTH CAROLINA

South Carolina Bar
950 Taylor Street
PO Box 608
Columbia, SC 29202
(803) 799-6653
http://www.scbar.org

SOUTH DAKOTA

State Bar of South Dakota
222 East Capitol
Pierre, SD 57501
(605) 224-7554
http://www.sdbar.org

TENNESSEE

Tennessee Bar Assn
3622 West End Avenue
Nashville, TN 37205
(615) 383-7421
http://www.tba.org

TEXAS

State Bar of Texas
1414 Colorado
PO Box 12487
Austin, TX 78711
(512) 463-1463
*http://www.texasbar.com/
start.htm*

UTAH

Utah State Bar
645 South 200 East, Suite 310
Salt Lake City, UT 84111
(801) 531-9077
http://www.utahbar.org

VERMONT

Vermont Bar Association
PO Box 100
Montpelier, VT 05601
(802) 223-2020
http://www.vtbar.org

VIRGINIA

Virginia State Bar
707 East Main Street, suite 1500
Richmond, VA 23219-0501
(804) 775-0500

Virginia Bar Association
701 East Franklin St., Suite 1120
Richmond, VA 23219
(804) 644-0041
http://www.vbar.org

VIRGIN ISLANDS

Virgin Islands Bar Association
P.O. Box 4108
Christiansted, Virgin Islands
00822
(340) 778-7497

WASHINGTON

Washington State Bar
Association
500 Westin Street
2001 Sixth Avenue
Seattle, WA 98121-2599
(206) 727-8200
http://www.wsba.org

WEST VIRGINIA

West Virginia State Bar
2006 Kanawha Blvd. East
Charleston, WV 25311
(304) 558-2456
http://www.wvbar.org

West Virginia Bar Association
904 Security Building
100 Capitol Street
Charleston, WV 25301
(304) 342-1474

WISCONSIN

State Bar of Wisconsin
402 West Wilson Street
Madison, WI 53703
(608) 257-3838
http://www.wisbar.org/
home.htm

WYOMING

Wyoming State Bar
500 Randall Avenue
Cheyenne, WY 82001
PO Box 109
Cheyenne, WY 82003
(307) 632-9061
http://www.wyomingbar.org

Appendix:

State requirements for Small Claims Court

STATE	DOLLAR LIMIT[a]	NAME OF COURT	WHERE TO SUE	SERVICE OF PROCESS	EVICTION
Alabama	$3,000	District Court	District where defendant lives	1) Sheriff 2) Process Server 3) Certified mail	No
Alaska	$7,500	Small Claims Court	Court nearest defendant	1) Peace officer 2) Process Server 3) Where applicable, registered or certified mail, through clerk	Yes
Arizona	$2,500	Small Claims Division of Justice of the Peace Court	Precinct where defendant lives	1) Sheriff 2) Process Server 3) First class, registered or certified mail	Allowed regular Justice Court
Arkansas	$5,000	Small Claims Division of Municipal Court	County where defendant lives	1) Sheriff 2) Process Server 3) Where applicable, certified mail	
California	$5,000 ($2,500 for suits involving a surety company)	Small Claims Court	District where defendant resides or resided when promise was made	1) Disinterested adult 2) Certified or registered mail	No
Colorado	$5,000	County Court, Small Claims Division	County where defendant lives or works	1) Sheriff 2) Disinterested adult 3) Certified or registered mail	No
Connecticut	$2,500	Small Claims Court	County where defendant resides	1) Regular mail, through clerk 2) Sheriff	No

a - Dollar limit is exclusive of interest and cost

STATE	DOLLAR LIMIT[a]	NAME OF COURT	WHERE TO SUE	SERVICE OF PROCESS	EVICTION
Delaware	$15,000	Justice of the Peace	Anywhere in the state	1) Sheriff 2) Coroner, Constable, Deputy Sheriff	Yes
District of Columbia	$5,000	Superior Court or Small Claims Court	There is only one court in D.C.	1) U.S. Marshall 2) Disinterested adult 3) Certified or registered mail	No
Florida	$5,000	County Court, Summary Procedure Division	County where defendant lives	1) Sheriff 2) Process Server 3) Certified mail	Yes
Georgia	$5,000	Magistrate Courts	County where defendant lives	1) Sheriff 2) Marshall of Court 3) Deputy 4) Person appointed by Court	Yes
Hawaii	$3,500 (no limit in landlord-tenant deposit cases; counterclaims up to $20,000)	District Court, Small Claims Division	Judicial district where defendant lives	1) Registered or certified mail, return receipt 2) Sheriff, Deputy, Chief of Police 3) Person appointed by Court	No
Idaho	$3,000	Small Claims Department of Magistrate's Division	County where defendant lives or where the claim arose	1) Sheriff, Deputy, Constable 2) Disinterested adult	No
Illinois	$5,000 ($2,500 in Cook County "Pro Se")	Small Claims Court	County where defendant lives or where claim arose	1) Sheriff, Deputy 2) Process Server 3) Certified mail	No
Indiana	$3,000 ($6,000 in Marion county)	Small Claims Court	County where defendant lives or where claim arose	1) Sheriff, Deputy 2) Person appointed by court 3) Registered or certified mail	Yes
Iowa	$4,000	Small Claims Court	County where defendant lives or where claim arose	1) Certified mail 2) Restricted delivery 3) Peace officer 4) Person appointed by Court	Yes

STATE	DOLLAR LIMIT[a]	NAME OF COURT	WHERE TO SUE	SERVICE OF PROCESS	EVICTION
Kansas	$1,800	Kansas Small Claims Court	County where defendant lives	1) Sheriff 2) Certified mail 3) Process Server	No
Kentucky	$1,500	Small Claims Court	County where defendant lives	1) Certified mail 2) Sheriff 3) Specified Bailiff appointed by Court	Yes
Louisiana	$2,000	Justice of the Peace Court	Parish where defendant lives	1) Sheriff 2) Constable 3) Person appointed by Court	Yes
Maine	$4,500	Small Claims Court	County where defendant lives	1) Sheriff 2) Deputy Sheriff 3) Process Server	Yes
Maryland	$2,500	District Court	County where defendant lives	1) Sheriff 2) Deputy Sheriff 3) Disinterested adult 4) Attorney of record	Yes
Massachusetts	$2,000 (no limit for property damage caused by a vehicle)	District Court	District where defendant or plaintiff resides	1) Registered mail 2) Sheriff 3) Deputy Sheriff 4) Person appointed by Court.	No
Michigan	$1,750	District Court	County where defendant lives or where claim arose	Disinterested adult	No
Minnesota	$7,500 ($4,000 for commercial plaintiff)	Conciliation Court	County where defendant lives	1) Sheriff 2) Disinterested adult	No
Mississippi	$2,500	Justice Court	County where defendant lives	1) Sheriff 2) Disinterested adult	No
Missouri	$3,000	Small Claims Court	County where defendant lives	1) Certified mail 2) Sheriff or Deputy 3) Coroner or Process Server	No

STATE	DOLLAR LIMIT[a]	NAME OF COURT	WHERE TO SUE	SERVICE OF PROCESS	EVICTION
Montana	$3,000	Small Claims Court	County where defendant lives	1) Sheriff or Deputy 2) Constable or disinterested adult	No
Nebraska	$2,100	County Court	County where defendant lives	1) Certified mail 2) Sheriff 3) Person authorized by law 4) Person appointed by Court	No
Nevada	$3,500	Justice's Court for Small Claims	City where defendant lives	1) Sheriff or Deputy 2) Disinterested adult	No
New Hampshire	$5,000	Small Claims Court	District where defendant or plaintiff resides	1) Registered mail 2) Sheriff or deputy	No
New Jersey	$2,000	Superior Court, Special Civil Division	County where defendant resides	1) Sheriff 2) Sergeant-at-arms 3) Person appointed by Court	No
New Mexico	$5,000	Magistrate Court, Small Claims Division	County where defendant can be found	1) Sheriff 2) Disinterested adult	Yes
New York	$3,000	Small Claims Court	County where defendant lives	1) Sheriff or Town Marshall 2) Process Server	No
North Carolina	$3,000	Small Claims Court	County where defendant lives	1) Sheriff or Town Marshall 2) Process Server	Yes
North Dakota	$5,000	Small Claims Court of County Court	County where defendant lives	Disinterested adult	No
Ohio	$3,000 ($5,000 in County Court)	Small Claims Court	County where defendant lives	1) Sheriff 2) Person appointed by Court	No
Oklahoma	$4,500	Small Claims Court of the District Court	County where defendant lives	1) Certified mail, return receipt 2) Sheriff 3) Process Server 4) Person appointed by Court	No

STATE	DOLLAR LIMIT[a]	NAME OF COURT	WHERE TO SUE	SERVICE OF PROCESS	EVICTION
Oregon	$3,500	District Court, Small Claims Division	Where defendant lives	1) Certified mail 2) Disinterested adult	No
Pennsylvania	$5,000	Magistrate Court	Where defendant can be served	Sheriff or Coroner	Yes
Rhode Island	$1,500	Small Claims Court of the District Court		1) Registered mail 2) Certified mail 3) Sheriff or Deputy 4) Town Sergeant 5) Constable	No
South Carolina	$5,000	Magistrate's Court	County where defendant lives	1) Sheriff or Deputy 2) Disinterested adult	Yes
South Dakota	$4,000	Small Claims Court	County where defendant lives	1) Certified mail 2) Sheriff or constable 3) Disinterested elector of County	No
Tennessee	$15,000 ($25,000 in larger counties or to recover personal property)	Courts of General Session	District where defendant lives	1) Sheriff or Deputy 2) Process Server 3) Certified mail, return receipt requested	Yes
Texas	$5,000	Small Claims Court	Precinct in which the defendant lives	1) Sheriff or Constable 2) Disinterested adult	No
Utah	$5,000	Small Claims Department of Circuit Court	County where defendant lives or where claim arose	1) Disinterested adult over 21 2) Sheriff	No
Vermont	$3,500		County where either party lives	1) Registered mail 2) Sheriff or Deputy 3) Constable 4) Person appointed by Court	No
Virginia	$3,000-$15,000 (check with county clerk)	Small Claims Court in Fairfax and Arlington counties Circuit Court in other counties.	District where defendant lives or where claim arose	1) Officer 2) Disinterested adult	Yes

STATE	DOLLAR LIMIT[a]	NAME OF COURT	WHERE TO SUE	SERVICE OF PROCESS	EVICTION
Washington	$2,500	District Court	County where defendant lives	1) Sheriff or Deputy 2) Disinterested adult	No
West Virginia	$5,000	County Magistrate's Court	County where defendant lives or where claim arose	1) Sheriff 2) Disinterested adult	Yes
Wisconsin	$5,000	Small Claims Court	County where defendant lives or claim arose	1) Service by certified mail if defendant is county resident 2) Disinterested adult	Yes
Wyoming	$4,000	County Court Small Claims Division	County where defendant lives	1) Registered mail 2) Sheriff or Deputy 3) Disinterested adult over 21	Yes

How to save on attorney fees

How to save on attorney fees

Millions of Americans know they need legal protection, whether it's to get agreements in writing, protect themselves from lawsuits, or document business transactions. But too often these basic but important legal matters are neglected because of something else millions of Americans know: legal services are expensive.

They don't have to be. In response to the demand for affordable **legal** protection and services, there are now specialized clinics that process simple documents. Paralegals help people prepare legal claims on a freelance basis. People find they can handle their own legal affairs with do-it-yourself legal **guides** and kits. Indeed, this book is a part of this growing trend.

When are these alternatives to a lawyer appropriate? If you hire **an attorney,** how can you make sure you're getting good advice for a reasonable fee? Most importantly, do you know how to lower your legal expenses?

When there is no alternative

Make no mistake: serious legal matters require a lawyer. The tips in this book can help you reduce your legal fees, but there is no alternative to good professional legal services in certain circumstances:

- when you are charged with a felony, you are a repeat offender, or jail is possible

- when a substantial amount of money or property is at stake in a lawsuit

- when you are a party in an adversarial divorce or custody case

- when you are an alien facing deportation

- when you are the plaintiff in a personal injury suit that involves large sums of money

- when you're involved in very important transactions

Are you sure you want to take it to court?

Consider the following questions before you pursue legal action:

What are your financial resources?

Money buys experienced attorneys, and experience wins over first-year lawyers and public defenders. Even with a strong case, you may save money by not going to court. Yes, people win millions in court. But for every big winner there are ten plaintiffs who either lose or win so little that litigation wasn't worth their effort.

Do you have the time and energy for a trial?

Courts are overbooked, and by the time your case is heard your initial zeal may have grown cold. If you can, make a reasonable settlement out of court. On personal matters, like a divorce or custody case, consider the emotional toll on all parties. Any legal case will affect you in some way. You will need time away from work. A newsworthy case may bring press coverage. Your loved ones, too, may face publicity. There is usually good reason to settle most cases quickly, quietly, and economically.

How can you settle disputes without litigation?

Consider *mediation*. In mediation, each party pays half the mediator's fee and, together, they attempt to work out a compromise informally. *Binding arbitration* is another alternative. For a small fee, a trained specialist serves as judge, hears both sides, and hands down a ruling that both parties have agreed to accept.

So you need an attorney

Having done your best to avoid litigation, if you still find yourself headed for court, you will need an attorney. To get the right attorney at a reasonable cost, be guided by these four questions:

What type of case is it?

You don't seek a foot doctor for a toothache. Find an attorney experienced in your type of legal problem. If you can get recommendations from clients who have recently won similar cases, do so.

Where will the trial be held?

You want a lawyer familiar with that court system and one who knows the court personnel and the local protocol—which can vary from one locality to another.

Should you hire a large or small firm?

Hiring a senior partner at a large and prestigious law firm sounds reassuring, but chances are the actual work will be handled by associates—at high rates. Small firms may give your case more attention but, with fewer resources, take longer to get the work done.

What can you afford?

Hire an attorney you can afford, of course, but know what a fee quote includes. High fees may reflect a firm's luxurious offices, high-paid staff and unmonitored expenses, while low estimates may mean "unexpected" costs later. Ask for a written estimate of all costs and anticipated expenses.

How to find a good lawyer

Whether you need an attorney quickly or you're simply open to future possibilities, here are seven nontraditional methods for finding your lawyer:

1) **Word of mouth**: Successful lawyers develop reputations. Your friends, business associates and other professionals are potential referral sources. But beware of hiring a friend. Keep the client-attorney relationship strictly business.

2) **Directories**: The Yellow Pages and the Martin-Hubbell Lawyer Directory (in your local library) can help you locate a lawyer with the right education, background and expertise for your case.

3) **Databases**: A paralegal should be able to run a quick computer search of local attorneys for you using the Westlaw or Lexis database.

4) **State bar associations**: Bar associations are listed in phone books. Along with lawyer referrals, your bar association can direct you to low-cost legal clinics or specialists in your area.

5) **Law schools**: Did you know that a legal clinic run by a law school gives law students hands-on experience? This may fit your legal needs. A third-year law student loaded with enthusiasm and a little experience might fill the bill quite inexpensively—or even for free.

6) **Advertisements**: Ads are a lawyer's business card. If a "TV attorney" seems to have a good track record with your kind of case, why not call? Just don't be swayed by the glamour of a high-profile attorney.

7) **Your own ad**: A small ad describing the qualifications and legal expertise you're seeking, placed in a local bar association journal, may get you just the lead you need.

How to hire and work with your attorney

No matter how you hear about an attorney, you must interview him or her in person. Call the office during business hours and ask to speak to the attorney directly. Then explain your case briefly and mention how you obtained the attorney's name. If the attorney sounds interested and knowledgeable, arrange for a visit.

The ten-point visit

1) Note the address. This is a good indication of the rates to expect.

2) Note the condition of the offices. File-laden desks and poorly maintained work space may indicate a poorly run firm.

3) Look for up-to-date computer equipment and an adequate complement of support personnel.

4) Note the appearance of the attorney. How will he or she impress a judge or jury?

5) Is the attorney attentive? Does the attorney take notes, ask questions, follow up on points you've mentioned?

6) Ask what schools he or she has graduated from, and feel free to check credentials with the state bar association.

7) Does the attorney have a good track record with your type of case?

8) Does he or she explain legal terms to you in plain English?

9) Are the firm's costs reasonable?

10) Will the attorney provide references?

Hiring the attorney

Having chosen your attorney, make sure all the terms are agreeable. Send letters to any other attorneys you have interviewed, thanking them for their time and interest in your case and explaining that you have retained another attorney's services.

Request a letter from your new attorney outlining your retainer agreement. The letter should list all fees you will be responsible for as well as the billing arrangement. Did you arrange to pay in installments? This should be noted in your retainer agreement.

Controlling legal costs

Legal fees and expenses can get out of control easily, but the client who is willing to put in the effort can keep legal costs manageable. Work out a budget with your attorney. Create a timeline for your case. Estimate the costs involved in each step.

Legal fees can be straightforward. Some lawyers charge a fixed rate for a specific project. Others charge contingency fees (they collect a percentage of your recovery, usually 35-50 percent if you win and nothing if you lose). But most attorneys prefer to bill by the hour. Expenses can run the gamut, with one hourly charge for taking depositions and another for making copies.

Have your attorney give you a list of charges for services rendered and an itemized monthly bill. The bill should explain the service performed, who performed the work, when the service was provided, how long it took, and how the service benefits your case.

Ample opportunity abounds in legal billing for dishonesty and greed. There is also plenty of opportunity for knowledgeable clients to cut their bills significantly if they know what to look for. Asking the right questions and setting limits on fees is smart and can save you a bundle. Don't be afraid to question legal bills. It's your case and your money!

When the bill arrives

- **Retainer fees**: You should already have a written retainer agreement. Ideally, the retainer fee applies toward case costs, and your agreement puts that in writing. Protect yourself by escrowing the retainer fee until the case has been handled to your satisfaction.

- **Office visit charges**: Track your case and all documents, correspondence, and bills. Diary all dates, deadlines and questions you want to ask your attorney during your next office visit. This keeps expensive office visits focused and productive, with more accomplished in less time. If your attorney charges less for phone consultations than office visits, reserve visits for those tasks that must be done in person.

- **Phone bills**: This is where itemized bills are essential. Who made the call, who was spoken to, what was discussed, when was the call made, and how long did it last? Question any charges that seem unnecessary or excessive (over 60 minutes).

- **Administrative costs**: Your case may involve hundreds, if not thousands, of documents: motions, affidavits, depositions, interrogatories, bills, memoranda, and letters. Are they all necessary? Understand your attorney's case strategy before paying for an endless stream of costly documents.

- **Associate and paralegal fees**: Note in your retainer agreement which staff people will have access to your file. Then you'll have an informed and efficient staff working on your case, and you'll recognize their names on your bill. Of course, your attorney should handle the important part of your case, but less costly paralegals or associates may handle routine matters more economically. Note: Some firms expect their associates to meet a quota of billable hours, although the time spent is not always warranted. Review your bill. Does the time spent make sense for the document in question? Are several staff involved in matters that should be handled by one person? Don't be afraid to ask questions. And withhold payment until you have satisfactory answers.

- **Court stenographer fees**: Depositions and court hearings require costly transcripts and stenographers. This means added expenses. Keep an eye on these costs.

- **Copying charges**: Your retainer fee should limit the number of copies made of your complete file. This is in your legal interest, because multiple files mean multiple chances others may access your confidential information. It is also in your financial interest, because copying costs can be astronomical.

- **Fax costs**: As with the phone and copier, the fax can easily run up costs. Set a limit.

- **Postage charges**: Be aware of how much it costs to send a legal document overnight, or a registered letter. Offer to pick up or deliver expensive items when it makes sense.

- **Filing fees**: Make it clear to your attorney that you want to minimize the number of court filings in your case. Watch your bill and question any filing that seems unnecessary.

- **Document production fee**: Turning over documents to your opponent is mandatory and expensive. If you're faced with reproducing boxes of documents, consider having the job done by a commercial firm rather than your attorney's office.

- **Research and investigations**: Pay only for photographs that can be used in court. Can you hire a photographer at a lower rate than what your attorney charges? Reserve that right in your retainer agreement. Database research can also be extensive and expensive; if your attorney uses Westlaw or Nexis, set limits on the research you will pay for.

- **Expert witnesses**: Question your attorney if you are expected to pay for more than a reasonable number of expert witnesses. Limit the number to what is essential to your case.

- **Technology costs**: Avoid videos, tape recordings, and graphics if you can use old-fashioned diagrams to illustrate your case.

- **Travel expenses**: Travel expenses for those connected to your case can be quite costly unless you set a maximum budget. Check all travel-related items on your bill, and make sure they are appropriate. Always question why the travel is necessary before you agree to pay for it.

- **Appeals costs**: Losing a case often means an appeal, but weigh the costs involved before you make that decision. If money is at stake, do a cost-benefit analysis to see if an appeal is financially justified.

- **Monetary damages**: Your attorney should be able to help you estimate the total damages you will have to pay if you lose a civil case. Always consider settling out of court rather than proceeding to trial when the trial costs will be high.

- **Surprise costs**: Surprise costs are so routine they're predictable. The judge may impose unexpected court orders on one or both sides, or the opposition will file an unexpected motion that increases your legal costs. Budget a few thousand dollars over what you estimate your case will cost. It usually is needed.

- **Padded expenses**: Assume your costs and expenses are legitimate. But some firms do inflate expenses—office supplies, database searches, copying, postage, phone bills—to bolster their bottom line. Request copies of bills your law firm receives from support services. If you are not the only client represented on a bill, determine those charges related to your case.

Keeping it legal without a lawyer

The best way to save legal costs is to avoid legal problems. There are hundreds of ways to decrease your chances of lawsuits and other nasty legal encounters. Most simply involve a little common sense. You can also use your own initiative to find and use the variety of self-help legal aid available to consumers.

11 situations in which you may not need a lawyer

1) **No-fault divorce**: Married couples with no children, minimal property, and no demands for alimony can take advantage of divorce mediation services. A lawyer should review your divorce agreement before you sign it, but you will have saved a fortune in attorney fees. A marital or family counselor may save a seemingly doomed marriage, or help both parties move beyond anger to a calm settlement. Either way, counseling can save you money.

2) **Wills**: Do-it-yourself wills and living trusts are ideal for people with estates of less than $600,000. Even if an attorney reviews your final documents, a will kit allows you to read the documents, ponder your bequests, fill out sample forms, and discuss your wishes with your family at your leisure, without a lawyer's meter running.

3) **Incorporating**: Incorporating a small business can be done by any business owner. Your state government office provides the forms and instructions necessary. A visit to your state office will probably be

necessary to perform a business name check. A fee of $100-$200 is usually charged for processing your Articles of Incorporation. The rest is paperwork: filling out forms correctly; holding regular, official meetings; and maintaining accurate records.

4) **Routine business transactions**: Copyrights, for example, can be applied for by asking the U.S. Copyright Office for the appropriate forms and brochures. The same is true of the U.S. Patent and Trademark Office. If your business does a great deal of document preparation and research, hire a certified paralegal rather than paying an attorney's rates. Consider mediation or binding arbitration rather than going to court for a business dispute. Hire a human resources/benefits administrator to head off disputes concerning discrimination or other employee charges.

5) **Repairing bad credit**: When money matters get out of hand, attorneys and bankruptcy should not be your first solution. Contact a credit counseling organization that will help you work out manageable payment plans so that everyone wins. It can also help you learn to manage your money better. A good company to start with is the Consumer Credit Counseling Service, 1-800-388-2227.

6) **Small Claims Court**: For legal grievances amounting to a few thousand dollars in damages, represent yourself in Small Claims Court. There is a small filing fee, forms to fill out, and several court visits necessary. If you can collect evidence, state your case in a clear and logical presentation, and come across as neat, respectful and sincere, you can succeed in Small Claims Court.

7) **Traffic Court**: Like Small Claims Court, Traffic Court may show more compassion to a defendant appearing without an attorney. If you are ticketed for a minor offense and want to take it to court, you will be asked to plead guilty or not guilty. If you plead guilty, you can ask for leniency in sentencing by presenting mitigating circumstances. Bring any witnesses who can support your story, and remember that presentation (some would call it acting ability) is as important as fact.

8) **Residential zoning petition**: If a homeowner wants to open a home business, build an addition, or make other changes that may affect his or her neighborhood, town approval is required. But you don't need a lawyer to fill out a zoning variance application, turn it in, and present your story at a public hearing. Getting local support before the hearing is the best way to assure a positive vote; contact as many neighbors as possible to reassure them that your plans won't adversely affect them or the neighborhood.

9) **Government benefit applications**: Applying for veterans' or unemployment benefits may be daunting, but the process doesn't require legal help. Apply for either immediately upon becoming eligible. Note: If your former employer contests your application for unemployment benefits and you have to defend yourself at a hearing, you may want to consider hiring an attorney.

10) **Receiving government files**: The Freedom of Information Act gives every American the right to receive copies of government information about him or her. Write a letter to the appropriate state or federal agency, noting the precise information you want. List each document in a separate paragraph. Mention the Freedom of Information Act, and state that you will pay any expenses. Close with your signature and the address the documents should be sent to. An approved request may take six months to arrive. If it is refused on the grounds that the information is classified or violates another's privacy, send a letter of appeal explaining why the released information would not endanger anyone. Enlist the support of your local state or federal representative, if possible, to smooth the approval process.

11) **Citizenship**: Arriving in the United States to work and become a citizen is a process tangled in bureaucratic red tape, but it requires more perseverance than legal assistance. Immigrants can learn how to obtain a "Green Card," under what circumstances they can work, and what the requirements of citizenship are by contacting the Immigration Services or reading a good self-help book.

Save more; it's E-Z

When it comes to saving attorneys' fees, E-Z Legal Forms is the consumer's best friend. America's largest publisher of self-help legal products offers legally valid forms for virtually every situation. E-Z Legal Kits and E-Z Legal Guides include all necessary forms with a simple-to-follow manual of instructions or a layman's book. E-Z Legal Books are a legal library of forms and documents for everyday business and personal needs. E-Z Legal Software provides those same forms on disk and CD for customized documents at the touch of the keyboard.

You can add to your legal savvy and your ability to protect yourself, your loved ones, your business and your property with a range of self-help legal titles available through E-Z Legal Forms. See the product descriptions and information at the back of this guide.

Whatever you need to know, we've made it E-Z!

Informative text and forms you can fill out on-screen.* From personal to business, legal to leisure—we've made it E-Z!

PERSONAL & FAMILY

For all your family's needs, we have titles that will help keep you organized and guide you through most every aspect of your personal life.

BUSINESS

Whether you're starting from scratch with a home business or you just want to keep your corporate records in shape, we've got the programs for you.

* Not all topics include forms   ss 1999.r2

FEDERAL & STATE
Labor Law Posters

The Poster 15 Million Businesses Must Have This Year!

All businesses must display federal labor laws at each location, or risk fines and penalties of up to $7,000!
And changes in September and October of 1997 made all previous Federal Labor Law Posters obsolete;
so make sure you're in compliance—use ours!

State	Item#	State	Item#	State	Item#
Alabama	83801	Louisiana	83818	Ohio	83835
Alaska	83802	Maine	83819	Oklahoma	83836
Arizona	83803	Maryland	83820	Oregon	83837
Arkansas	83804	Massachusetts	83821	Pennsylvania	83838
California	83805	Michigan	83822	Rhode Island	83839
Colorado	83806	Minnesota	83823	South Carolina	83840
Connecticut	83807	Mississippi	83824	*South Dakota not available*	
Delaware	83808	Missouri	83825	Tennessee	83842
Florida	83809	Montana	83826	Texas	83843
Georgia	83810	Nebraska	83827	Utah	83844
Hawaii	83811	Nevada	83828	Vermont	83845
Idaho	83812	New Hampshire	83829	Virginia	83846
Illinois	83813	New Jersey	83830	Washington	83847
Indiana	83814	New Mexico	83831	Washington, D.C.	83848
Iowa	83815	New York	83832	West Virginia	83849
Kansas	83816	North Carolina	83833	Wisconsin	83850
Kentucky	83817	North Dakota	83834	Wyoming	83851

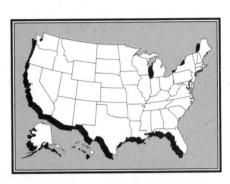

State Labor Law Compliance Poster

Avoid up to $10,000 in fines by posting the
required State Labor Law Poster available from
Made E-Z Products.

$29.95

ss1999.r2

Federal Labor Law Poster

This colorful, durable 17³/₄" x 24" poster is in
full federal compliance and includes:

- The NEW Fair Labor Standards Act Effective
  October 1, 1996
  (New Minimum Wage Act)

- The Family & Medical Leave Act of 1993*

- The Occupational Safety and Health
  Protection Act of 1970

- The Equal Opportunity Act

- The Employee Polygraph Protection Act

* Businesses with fewer than 50 employees should display reverse
side of poster, which excludes this act.

$11.99
Stock No. LP001

See the order form in this guide to order yours today!

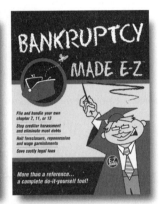

	Item#	Qty.	Price Ea.‡
★ **E•Z Legal Kits**			
Bankruptcy	K100		$23.95
Incorporation	K101		$23.95
Divorce	K102		$29.95
Credit Repair	K103		$21.95
Living Trust	K105		$21.95
Living Will	K106		$23.95
Last Will & Testament	K107		$18.95
Buying/Selling Your Home	K111		$21.95
Employment Law	K112		$21.95
Collecting Child Support	K115		$21.95
Limited Liability Company	K116		$21.95
★ **Made E•Z Software**			
Accounting Made E-Z	SW1207		$29.95
Asset Protection Made E-Z	SW1157		$29.95
Bankruptcy Made E-Z	SW1154		$29.95
Best Career Oppportunities Made E-Z	SW1216		$29.95
Brain-Buster Crossword Puzzles	SW1223		$29.95
Brain-Buster Jigsaw Puzzles	SW1222		$29.95
Business Startups Made E-Z	SW1192		$29.95
Buying/Selling Your Home Made E-Z	SW1213		$29.95
Car Buying Made E-Z	SW1146		$29.95
Corporate Record Keeping Made E-Z	SW1159		$29.95
Credit Repair Made E-Z	SW1153		$29.95
Divorce Law Made E-Z	SW1182		$29.95
Everyday Law Made E-Z	SW1185		$29.95
Everyday Legal Forms & Agreements	SW1186		$29.95
Incorporation Made E-Z	SW1176		$29.95
Last Wills Made E-Z	SW1177		$29.95
Living Trusts Made E-Z	SW1178		$29.95
Offshore Investing Made E-Z	SW1218		$29.95
Owning a Franchise Made E-Z	SW1202		$29.95
Touring Florence, Italy Made E-Z	SW1220		$29.95
Touring London, England Made E-Z	SW1221		$29.95
Vital Record Keeping Made E-Z	SW1160		$29.95
Website Marketing Made E-Z	SW1203		$29.95
Your Profitable Home Business	SW1204		$29.95
★ **Made E•Z Guides**			
Bankruptcy Made E-Z	G200		$17.95
Incorporation Made E-Z	G201		$17.95
Divorce Law Made E-Z	G202		$17.95
Credit Repair Made E-Z	G203		$17.95
Living Trusts Made E-Z	G205		$17.95
Living Wills Made E-Z	G206		$17.95
Last Wills Made E-Z	G207		$17.95
Small Claims Court Made E-Z	G209		$17.95
Traffic Court Made E-Z	G210		$17.95
Buying/Selling Your Home Made E-Z	G211		$17.95
Employment Law Made E-Z	G212		$17.95
Collecting Child Support Made E-Z	G215		$17.95
Limited Liability Companies Made E-Z	G216		$17.95
Partnerships Made E-Z	G218		$17.95
Solving IRS Problems Made E-Z	G219		$17.95
Asset Protection Secrets Made E-Z	G220		$17.95
Immigration Made E-Z	G223		$17.95
Buying/Selling a Business Made E-Z	G223		$17.95
★ **Made E•Z Books**			
Managing Employees Made E-Z	BK308		$29.95
Corporate Record Keeping Made E-Z	BK310		$29.95
Vital Record Keeping Made E-Z	BK312		$29.95
Business Forms Made E-Z	BK313		$29.95
Collecting Unpaid Bills Made E-Z	BK309		$29.95
Everyday Law Made E-Z	BK311		$29.95
Everyday Legal Forms & Agreements	BK307		$29.95
★ **Labor Posters**			
Federal Labor Law Poster	LP001		$11.99
State Labor Law Poster (specify state)			$29.95
★ SHIPPING & HANDLING*			$
★ **TOTAL OF ORDER**:**			$

ss 1999.r2

Index